Encouraging Your Child's
Science Talent

Encouraging Your Child's
Science Talent

The Involved Parents' Guide

Michael S. **Matthews, Ph.D.**

Prufrock Press Inc.
Waco, Texas

© 2006 Prufrock Press Inc.
All Rights Reserved.
    Library of Congress Cataloging-in-Publication Data

Matthews, Michael S., 1968–
    Encouraging your child's science talent : the involved parents' guide
    / by Michael S. Matthews.
        p. cm.
    Includes bibliographical references.
    ISBN 1-59363-186-3 (pbk.)
    1. Science—Study and teaching (Elementary)—Parent participation.
    2. Science—Study and teaching (Secondary)—Parent participation.
    3. Science projects. I. Title.
    LB1585.M34 2006
    372.3'5—dc22

                            2005037611

Edited by Lacy Elwood
Layout and cover design by Marjorie Parker
ISBN-13: 978-1-59363-186-4
ISBN-10: 1-59363-186-3

At the time of this book's publication, all facts and figures cited are the most current available. All telephone numbers, addresses, and Web site URLs are accurate and active. All publications, organizations, Web sites, and other resources exist as described in the book, and all have been verified. The authors and Prufrock Press Inc., make no warranty or guarantee concerning the information and materials given out by organizations or content found at Web sites, and we are not responsible for any changes that occur after this book's publication. If you find an error, please contact Prufrock Press Inc. We strongly recommend to parents, teachers, and other adults that you monitor children's use of the Internet.

PRUFROCK PRESS INC.
P.O. Box 8813
Waco, Texas 76714-8813
(800) 998-2208
http://www.prufrock.com

This book is dedicated to my parents, Jan and Bob, who have provided many years of encouragement and inspiration.

Contents

— Chapter **5** —
Modifying Education for Your Scientifically Advanced Child

— Chapter **6** —
Helping Your Child With Science Fairs and Other Research-Based Competitions

— Chapter **7** —
The Big Picture: Thinking About the Future

— List of **Tables & Figures** —

Introduction

Many parents recognize the need for their children to excel in science, but are unsure how to promote this outcome. Even parents who have had extensive training in an area of science, or who work in a scientific field, may not be certain how to help their children develop both an interest and an ability in science. There can appear to be little connection between how children learn science and what adult scientists actually do. This book is designed to help bridge that gap, offering parents a framework within which they can develop their ability to support their child's scientific learning.

Why science? Scientific knowledge and ability is important far beyond career choices. It is vital in making appropriate personal and political decisions. As technology grows more complex and interrelated, everyone benefits from knowing as much as possible about scientific topics ranging from amino acids to zymurgy.

This book is specifically designed for you as a parent who wishes to do more to help your child excel in science learning.

Children who start ahead of the game in academic learning tend to stay ahead of their peers as they get older, provided they continue to receive appropriate educational experiences. The things you do to promote the development of your child's academic interests and achievements will provide him or her with a strong foundation on which to construct later learning.

This book is organized into seven chapters. Chapter 1 offers a brief introduction to what science and technology are and are not, Chapter 2 offers guidelines on how to recognize scientific ability in your child, and Chapter 3 discusses steps you can take at home to develop your child's abilities, offers suggestions for finding help in your community, and considers issues of special interest regarding scientifically able girls.

Chapter 4 offers advice on working with the school system to promote effective science learning for your child and others. This chapter also offers an overview of the two national curriculum standards for science teaching and learning, and tells how you as a parent can use these standards to support your child's education.

Chapter 5 suggests ways to modify your child's education to help him or her reach his or her full potential. Options such as charter schools, magnet schools, distance education, and home-schooling are included.

Chapter 6 leads you through ways to encourage your child's interest in independent science study, including detailed guidance on science fairs and science projects. Sections cover each part of science project development. Topic selection is particularly emphasized, because many students and parents seem to find this the most difficult aspect of doing an independent project.

Chapter 7 concludes this book with a look at the big picture. It summarizes steps for success, and suggests ways that the steps you take now will help your child throughout his or her life, regardless of whether he or she makes a career out of science.

I have based this book in large part on my own varied experiences as a science learner, science teacher, and parent. Many other experts have contributed to this effort indirectly, by authoring the resources cited throughout the volume. I hope this book suggests a variety of possibilities for you as a parent who wishes to encourage a child's successful pursuit of knowledge to consider. Above all, keep in mind that learning is much easier when it is also fun!

Chapter 1

What Science
Is—and Is Not

P erhaps you have already found a satisfying career in a scientific field such as medicine, geology, or engineering, and know from firsthand experience how important it is to develop your child's abilities so she can achieve similar success in science. Her interest is already evident, and you're simply looking for ways to effectively capitalize on it. Great! With a match like this, you're well on your way. Skim or skip this chapter, and move on to the ideas that follow.

But, what if you have little firsthand experience in scientific fields? Are you perplexed as to the best way to encourage your child in an area of study that has always totally mystified you? Or, are you perhaps a great proponent of scientific literacy for everyone, yet your child shows little interest?

Success can be yours, as well. Let's start at the beginning, and go from there, taking it for granted that you're an intelligent person, but not presupposing any prior science experience. Please don't think I'm patronizing you if I explain a term or concept you've known for years. I don't want to leave anyone out in the cold.

Conceptions and Misconceptions

We need to start here, so that you may recognize misconceptions when you encounter them. Many sources are available for further reading on these issues, and you can find a substantial amount of information by conducting a Web search on the relevant terms.

What Is Science, Really?

For too many people, the mere thought of science conjures up intimidating images of grim-faced men in white lab coats, solemnly muttering dire pronouncements in unintelligible jargon. Alternatively, they see ivory-tower dilettantes, one week telling us that something is bad for us, the next week telling us it is, after all, good. Science is seen as something very large, difficult to master, and in general, slightly threatening.

Why these negative stereotypes? Most arise because the general public—and unfortunately this includes many teachers—commonly hold several misconceptions about the nature of science. Viewing science as a set of immutable facts, they become confused or antagonistic when yesterday's fact seems to become today's fiction. Some go as far as to say they don't believe in science or in the facts of science.

Part of the problem is, undoubtedly, terminology. We'll tackle some of this terminology below, to help clear up some of these misconceptions.

Facts and the Scientific Method

The word *fact* has a number of meanings, including both "something that actually exists or has happened" and "a truth known by observation." Thus, scientific facts are both observations and judgments. In the second sense, they can be thought of as beliefs, but they are not the same as beliefs in religion. In science, facts as "truth" are built on repeated and repeatable observations. Anyone who wants to make the effort can repeat a scientific observation, even one that was first made hundreds of years ago (see, for example, Kipnis, 1993). Statements that cannot be tested through observation, such as spiritual beliefs, fall outside of the realm of science. For example, because no one can observe angels, the number of angels that can fit on the head of a pin is not a scientific question, but rather a theological one. Science limits itself to observable phenomena.

Science depends on a series of steps—usually called the *scientific method*—for evaluating claims about the world. By following the steps, anyone can develop new knowledge that represents an accurate description of his or her observations about the world, and present it in a form others can repeat. In the most basic form of the scientific method, observation and description lead to a preliminary explanation called a *hypothesis*—an informed guess about what has been observed. Based on this explanation, a prediction is made as to what will be observed next. Experimentation or further observation is used to see if what happens in the experiment or test stage will support or fail to support the hypothesis. If results fail to support this reasoned guess, one guesses again via a new or revised hypothesis.

Although science rarely matches this step-by-step process exactly, scientific inquiry often includes the posing and testing of hypotheses. It's a fairly straightforward process, but unfortunately a common source of confusion in the public's understand-

Table 1 **What Science Is—and Is Not**	
Science IS:	Science is NOT:
A way of understanding what one observes	An unchangeable set of facts (that's dogma!)
Evidence presented in a way that others can repeat	Statements that must be taken on faith (that's religion!)
Based on a special way of using words	Based on words used in the same way as the legal profession (that's law!)
Driven by the need to understand something about the observable world	Driven by the need to improve a task or product (that's technology!)

ing of science arises from the language used to describe the scientific method's outcomes. In everyday speech, the terms *hypothesis, law, theory,* and *model* are sometimes used interchangeably. However, in science, these refer to concepts with different degrees of support. The hypothesis is the weakest term in a sense, as it often is used to describe a preliminary guess; it is the suspected answer that guides the nature of the research addressing a particular question.

When a number of hypotheses about a phenomenon have been supported by observations, they may be combined into a generalized explanation called a *theory*. A theory is a large-scale hypothesis that has been supported by many observations. Theories usually are supported by more than one line of evidence, all leading to the same conclusion.

Because theories are well-supported by observations, the discovery of new conflicting data usually leads to revision rather than

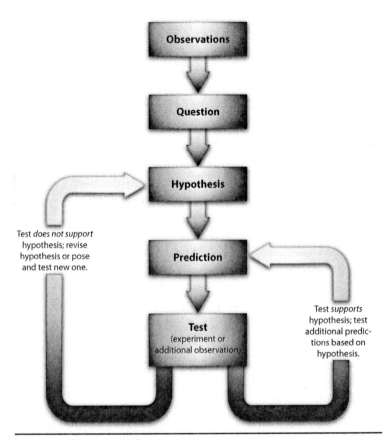

Figure 1. The scientific method

total disproof. Einstein's theory of relativity and Darwin's theory of evolution are examples of powerful theories. They satisfactorily explain the results of studies of a number of lesser hypotheses. However, because scientists view theories as explanations rather than as dogma, they continue to test each theory's limits.

A scientific law is a broadly applicable and extremely well-supported theory often simple enough to express as a single mathematical equation. The ideal gas law, which describes the relationship between the temperature, pressure, and volume of a gas, is a good example. However, even laws are not beyond disproof, and so scientific research continues to test their limits.

Another useful tool of scientific thinking is a model—a physical, mental, or mathematical representation of how people understand a process or idea. Because the term law implies something that holds true in every situation, the looser term model is sometimes used to refer to a law or theory after further work shows that it holds true under some circumstances, but not others. For example, back in the

> Theory is an explanation of how and why things happen. A law is an explanation of what things happen.

1600s, Isaac Newton successfully confirmed hypotheses that "objects in motion tend to remain in motion" and "objects at rest tend to remain at rest," and these observations became part of what is known as Newton's Laws of Motion. For about 300 years, these explanations have worked well for describing the behavior of things we can see. However, recent work has shown that at very small scales (the size of atoms), his rules no longer provide accurate predictions. Thus, some physicists now speak of Newton's laws as models.

Hypotheses supported by repeated experimentation eventually lead to the development of theories, which may eventually come to be regarded as laws; if further tests show they don't apply in some situations, they may later be called models. The following example shows how this all comes together.

Less than a century ago, continental drift was a new hypothesis and its originators were widely regarded as crackpots. Everyone else believed (theorized!) that continents had always been in the same places, and no one could imagine (hypothesize!) how something so large could move with no obvious forces pushing it. In the 1960s, the theory of continental drift found support when the theory of plate tectonics was developed to explain a mechanism that could move the continents. Today, we have the technology for direct measurements confirming the rates of movement of the continental plates. Because of these measurements, continental drift is now considered to be a fact, and plate tectonics is a well-accepted theory explaining how continental drift occurs.

How Are Science and Technology Related?

Many of the skills and methods of science and technology are quite similar, but they differ in their end goals. Strictly speaking, science seeks to produce new understandings about the world, without necessarily producing a practical result. Technology entails the application of this understanding to the improvement of a task or product. This distinction is more important in theory than in practice, because scientific research usually requires technological expertise in some area. Furthermore, technological progress often occurs prior to a full understanding of the scientific principles at work, and scientific advances may emerge in the course of technological development. Articles in the newsmagazine *Chemical Heritage* offer one excellent source of examples highlighting the interplay between science and technology.

How Is Science Best Taught to Children?

There may be more answers to this question than there are colleges of education in this country. At one time, the primary goal of science education was simply to instill a body of basic information into a student's mind. However, as both this body of knowledge and the data on how children learn have grown, the thinking generally has changed among science educators. Two teaching approaches have been found to be particularly effective: holistic instruction and inquiry-based instruction. The two approaches are not mutually exclusive, but in fact complement each other nicely.

Particularly popular at the elementary school level, *holistic instruction* is cross-disciplinary instruction that integrates scientific content with areas such as art, literature, drama, history, and mathematics. Literature is often used as a springboard for scientific instruction, and writing skills are emphasized. For an example of holistic instruction, see the Great Explorations in Math and Science (GEMS) program's *Connecting Young People's Literature to Great Explorations in Math and Science*, published in 1993 by Lawrence Hall of Science.

Inquiry-based instruction is founded on the judgment that there now seems to be just too much scientific information for any one person to master simply by rote memorization. Thus, it is more important to emphasize teaching the skills and attributes students need to actively obtain and evaluate scientific information on their own. The most effective approach to doing this seems to be through exploratory activities with an element of inquiry. In other words, students seem to best develop attributes such as scientific curiosity and logical thinking by becoming involved in asking researchable questions, designing experiments, and communicating experimental results to their peers and teachers. For an example of inquiry-based instruction, see the American Association for the Advancement of Science's *Benchmarks for Science Literacy: Project 2061*, published in 1993 by Oxford University Press.

Happily, parents can utilize both of these approaches as well as or better than classroom teachers. The chapters that follow offer ideas to get you started.

Chapter 2

Assessing Your Child's Interest and Ability in Science so You Can Encourage More of Both

I t goes almost without saying that giving your child a happy home life, a stimulating environment, a superior diet, and the best of health care will help develop his or her potential for superior achievement in all aspects of life. Most of this book is about the additional things you, as a parent, can do to encourage your child to grow and develop in desirable ways, especially with regard to his or her interest and ability in science.

You know in your heart that your child is special; that's a major reason why you're reading this book. It's unrealistic, however, not to consider the influence of some real limits placed on your child. Some children just seem to be able to learn and comprehend complex situations more easily than others. In addition, your child's personality and intellect will certainly influence his responses to the things you do. It will be a lot easier on your child—and you—if you accept these predispositions and work with them instead of against them.

Knowledge really is power. Learn all you can about your child. This chapter suggests some ways to begin.

Identifying Your Child's Scientific Strengths

Theoretically, potential science talent should be easy to identify and encourage. Intuition says to simply look for the children who excel in science class in school, and reward them for doing so. To give them the best head start, evaluate and reward your children early and often.

Real life is often not that simple. For one thing, there may not be a science class in which young students can excel. In today's elementary schools, science occupies a middle ground with social studies, somewhere between the core subjects of language arts and mathematics and special (enrichment) classes like art, music, and physical education. Many schools appear to be retrenching their curricula, intensifying their focus on the core classes and doing away with as many of the additional subject areas as they can, particularly at the elementary levels (Solocheck, 2005). Recess is only a memory in some elementary schools, and programs for gifted students have also been cut to add additional instruction in math and reading across the board (Sternberg, 2004). While science instruction will never be eliminated, it may be pushed onto the back burner when schools perceive that other subjects are more important. (Chapters 4 and 5 provide some ideas for ways to cope with, and perhaps change, this situation.)

Furthermore, while some scientifically gifted children may stand out from an early age, others may be late bloomers who need your parental enthusiasm, encouragement, and expertise to reach their potential. How can you identify them?

Examining What You Already Know as a Parent

You probably know a great deal more than you realize about your child's interests and abilities in science. It's time to step back and assess the information, both informal and formal, that you already have on hand.

Watch Your Child Play

Does your child play games with science-related themes, such as pretending to be an astronaut or a paleontologist? Both interest and enjoyment clearly play a key role in the early development of talent (Bloom, 1985).

At times, children may have such a strong commitment to their current area of interest that they appear obsessive about it in comparison with other children their age. As long as their interests do not become physically or psychologically dangerous, don't worry too much if your child plays the same game or does the same activity constantly. When his or her curiosity is satisfied, sometimes within days and sometimes within months, your child will move on to the next great interest.

Observe your child's interests and level of enjoyment in each activity in the course of normal playtime routines. If your feel your child's interests are inappropriate, providing an environment that encourages your child to develop interests in particular content areas is possible and can be quite effective; later chapters will suggest ways to do this.

Table 2 presents a list of some characteristic behaviors that have been identified for students talented in science. Do you recognize your child within the behaviors on this list? Although particular interests may vary quite a bit over time, behaviors such as these tend to recur across a wide variety of interest areas.

You also may observe that your child develops or applies unusual problem-solving techniques, a valuable ability in many areas of human endeavor. The child who stacks up a pile of books to indirectly measure the height of the family cat—an animal that for some reason will not stand still near a 5-year-old bearing a yardstick—has developed an unusual, yet functional, solution to the problem posed by a skittish cat. Such behaviors are a readily observable component of creativity, and should be praised and encouraged whenever you may encounter them. The majority of young children are creative, but for a variety of reasons, their creative abilities often diminish as they grow older (Runco, 2004; Torrance 1968).

> Remember: Be positive . . . Creativity is much easier to discourage than it is to encourage.

Pay Attention to Teachers' Stories

You know your own child best, so trust your own instincts first. However, especially in the early years of your child's education when schools do little standardized testing, teachers' stories often will provide your second-best source of information about your child's interests and accomplishments. When you talk with your child's teacher, make a point of asking if your child has expressed any strong or unusual interests in activities related to science.

Table 2
Characteristics of Students Talented in Science

1. Uses numbers often when expressing ideas
2. Is unusually able to describe ideas about science in words
3. Expresses interest in science topics at a very young age
4. Perceives relationships among different parts of a situation
5. Shows curiosity about what makes things work
6. Displays a strong imagination for scientific things
7. Loves to make collections, which show a high level of organization and detail
8. Is willing to spend long periods of time working alone
9. Possesses high drive and persistence, even in the face of setbacks
10. Has better-than-average ability in reading and/or mathematics
11. Places importance on learning the proper names of things
12. Is willing to pass up games or other activities in favor of science learning
13. Enjoys telling stories about science, including science fiction
14. Shows creativity in projects about science
15. Is not content with explanations that other children readily accept for how things work
16. Seeks proof before accepting new explanations
17. Has a strong memory for details
18. Sees the big picture; can generalize from seemingly unrelated details
19. Is able to understand abstractions at a young age

At this age, traits such as unusual curiosity, creativity, or imagination in science-related activities may be early indicators of interest and ability. The child who constantly takes things apart to figure out how they work, or who tries to test her ideas about cause and effect by conducting her own experiments, is displaying nascent scientific skills that parents

> Keep a close eye on the budding scientist who decides to experiment!

and teachers can guide and develop. Be especially aware that young children are not conscious of the ramifications of their experimental investigations. A young, scientifically curious child who puts soap in the classroom aquarium probably wanted to find out whether his actions would make bubbles for the fish to play with, and was unaware that soap kills fish . . . but the fish are still dead!

Rely on More Than Grades

Grades may offer the most obvious evidence that your child is good in science, but grades have limitations (see Table 3). First, formal grades are not commonly assigned to students in the early years of school. Furthermore, even if an elementary school does assign grades, students may not receive a separate mark for science.

Also, keep in mind that grades represent performance averaged over several weeks or months. The student who excels in one specific area of scientific interest may receive a mediocre report card, simply because her exemplary performance in one science unit was brought down by lower scores in another unit that she found less captivating. One way around this shortcoming is for parents to examine grades on classroom tests and projects, as these represent a shorter segment of the curriculum. A perceptive teacher may also share such information with parents.

Table 3
Rely on More Than Grades

Four reasons not to depend on grades alone in determining your child's science ability:
1. formal grades are not usually assigned in the early school years,
2. students may not have separate science classes or science grades,
3. students (particularly young ones) often vary in performance depending on interest in the topic, and
4. scientific interest may exhibit itself in unconventional ways unrelated to curriculum.

Finally, a child's classroom behavior in relation to the teacher's curriculum may reflect very little about his science abilities. Lists of traits of the scientifically inclined child that have been developed (Rakow, 1988, and others) include such factors as a questioning or investigative nature; above-average drive or persistence, particularly when faced with initial failure; and strong motor skills together with high mathematical and verbal abilities. At least one such list (Rakow) also includes activating factors, in the form of access to an appropriate learning environment and to a suitable teacher or mentor. Grade point averages are conspicuously missing from such lists.

Use Outside Information Wisely

Standardized tests, subject-specific tests, and talent searches are just some of the tools at your disposal as you work to help your child become successful in science. Each has its own role to play.

That being said, it's important not to come to speedy conclusions about your child's intelligence, particularly based on a limited indicator such as a test score. Illness, emotional upsets, and marked changes in environment are but some of the factors that can distort test results.

Understand the Strengths and Weaknesses of Standardized Tests

In one form or another, standardized tests measuring students' mastery of course content are now administered across the nation every year in grades 3–8. The term *standardized* refers to the fact that both the test itself and the testing conditions are the same for everyone. These standardized features include time limits, test directions, and question types. Although the specific questions vary from one version of a test to another, the overall format remains the same.

> Standardized = test time limits, directions, question types, and format are the same for everyone.

By ensuring the same conditions for all test takers, standardization increases the likelihood that score differences reflect real differences in students' capabilities rather than other unrelated factors (Matthews, 2004). Because standardized tests are used over a broad geographical area—usually state or nationwide—they offer the only defensible way of comparing student learning across different schools.

Standardized achievement tests are useful as general indicators of verbal or mathematical ability, but they provide little information specifically about abilities in science. Few of these tests have any science content, and even those that do tend to focus on basic rather than advanced knowledge. The science content of standardized tests tends to remain quite general until high school, which limits the usefulness of these tests for diagnostic purposes.

Parents should keep in mind that there are two varieties of standardized achievement tests. Each gives different information about your child's abilities. Table 4 describes these two types of tests.

Norm-referenced tests compare your child's test performance to other students of the same age and grade, letting you know whether your child is more able than other children. Norm-referenced scores are usually reported in the form of percentiles—numbers ranging from 1 to 99 that rank your child's performance relative to an average group of 100 similar students. The drawback of percentile scores is that once a score is at or above the 99th percentile, it does not tell you how far above this level your child may be capable of working. One way around this problem is to use an above-level test, such as those administered through talent search programs, which are discussed later in this chapter.

> Percentile = rank of your child relative to an average group of 100 similar students.

Other standardized tests are *criterion-referenced*. These measure student mastery of content knowledge, expressed by how many questions your child answered correctly on each part of the test (*raw scores*). Criterion-referenced tests can be useful for determining which of the content areas a child has mastered and which ones still need development. *Scale scores*, which use a mathematically transformed scale based on the raw scores, are used because they allow scores to be compared directly across different versions or different years of the same test.

Table 4 Basic Types of Standardized Achievement Tests	
Norm-Referenced Test	Criterion-Referenced Test
Compares your child's performance to that of other kids of the same age.	Measures how many of a set of questions your child can answer correctly (raw score).
Gives percentiles or a score that compares your child's score with other scores.	Gives scaled scores, which are used to determine achievement levels such as IV—Exceeds Expectations.
Helps identify how your child's test performance compares to the abilities of average students.	Helps identify areas your child has mastered and those still needing development.
Examples: Iowa Test of Basic Skills (ITBS), ACT, SAT, most IQ tests	Examples: Texas Assessment of Knowledge and Skills (TAKS™), New York Regents Test, high school graduation tests

In addition to standardized achievement tests, standardized intelligence tests are often used for the purpose of qualifying students to participate in the school's gifted program. The school's psychologist often is responsible for conducting testing for this purpose, and parents can request that their child be tested. Some schools will also accept results obtained from a private psychologist, although private individualized testing can become quite expensive.

While IQ testing can have the practical benefit of getting a child into a school's gifted program where science may be emphasized, it is important to realize that these tests measure only general abilities, often related to verbal and nonverbal (spatial, etc.) reasoning. Their results have only an indirect relationship to scientific ability, although strong verbal and spatial reasoning can be an asset in many fields of science and technology.

Use Local Tests to Strengthen Subject Mastery and Individualize Instruction

Unlike large standardized tests, tests at the classroom level, such as those given at the end of a chapter or unit of study, can be quite useful for assessment as early as the elementary years because they reveal the skills and areas of knowledge that a child is having difficulty mastering. For example, some children may need additional help with spelling, while others may benefit from greater attention to understanding ideas and interrelationships in the curriculum. Once children reach the upper elementary grades and beyond, subject-specific tests become more available, as well as more useful for assessment.

Classroom-level testing can also offer a readily available source of evidence about your student's preexisting knowledge of the curriculum. The best known of these approaches is perhaps Julian Stanley's DT-PI model (1978, 1998), which stands for *diagnostic testing* followed by *prescriptive instruction*; it was developed as a way to help students and teachers avoid redundancy in classroom instruction. In this model, all students in the class are given a pretest of the material in each instructional unit before the material is covered in class. Based on their pretest performance, any areas students have not yet mastered are taught rapidly until students can demonstrate that they have corrected these deficiencies. Students who have demonstrated mastery move on to work on learning more advanced concepts (similar material but in greater depth or breadth) while the rest of the class completes the regularly scheduled unit of instruction. Because the entire class can be given pretests in this manner, all students have an opportunity at the beginning of each unit to test out of the regular instruction. At the same time, students who usually test out of the material can take part in regular instruction with the rest of the class whenever necessary. The DT-PI approach has been shown to be effective with highly able students, particularly in mathematics.

Consider Talent Searches for High-Achieving Students

Talent searches provide another excellent option for students whose performance consistently falls at the top of the scale on classroom and grade-level standardized tests (Olszewski-Kubilius, 1998). The talent search model offers students whose scores are at the top of their grade level the opportunity to take an assessment test designed for students 3 to 5 years older. For example, fifth graders can take a test designed for eighth graders, and seventh graders can take a college admissions test usually given to high school juniors and seniors. Taking these more difficult tests shows how the abilities of students at the top of their class or school compare with similar students in other schools. For example, in the case of two students who have made perfect math scores on a grade level standardized test, the talent search test may show that one is two years ahead of his grade, while the other is five years ahead in math ability. Obviously these two students have quite different educational needs, even though the grade level test may have placed both in the 99th percentile.

There are four major talent search programs in the United States (see Table 5), as well as several smaller ones. All trace their origins to the work of psychologist Julian Stanley at Johns Hopkins University, but each program has developed somewhat different characteristics over the years. Each talent search pro-

---

Table 5
Four Major U.S. Talent Search Programs
for Advanced Students

- Talent Identification Program (TIP)
  Duke University, Durham, NC

- Center for Talented Youth (CTY)
  Johns Hopkins University, Baltimore, MD

- Rocky Mountain Talent Search
  University of Denver, Denver, CO

- Center for Talent Development (CTD)
  Northwestern University, Evanston, IL

---

gram focuses on students who live in a particular state or region. In addition to arranging testing, these programs typically also provide students and parents with resource materials, such as newsletters, and other enrichment programs, such as summer classes.

Talent searches offer a variety of educational opportunities, including distance learning classes, educational products, and summer and weekend educational programs. Although many of the talent search tests do not include a science component, the programs all offer a variety of science-related enrichment classes and materials. At Duke TIP, for example, recent summer program classes offered for grades 8–11 included aerospace engineering, introduction to medical science, and primate biology. Fifth-grade participants had an opportunity to spend a weekend studying the chemistry of light, or the math and physics of roller coasters. Interested students of any age can purchase a computer-based independent study unit on forensic science, *Clues in Crime*, from the program. Duke TIP is only one of several such programs, but these examples serve to illustrate how participation in a talent search program can be well worth the scientifically advanced child's time and effort.

Chapter 3

Supporting Your Scientifically Inclined Child at Home

Everyone is good at something but no one is good at everything. As this truism suggests, some of the most important things you can do as a parent are to help your child explore his or her strengths, whatever they may be, and discover what opportunities these abilities may lead toward. Whether you feel like you know a little or a lot about science, there are many ways in which you can be a tremendous help to your uniquely talented child. Many of these are good ideas to use with all children, but here I have suggested how they might benefit scientifically able children in particular.

Moving From Ability to Talent

Since at least the 1970s, and with increasing interest over the past decade, the education community has been carrying on a great deal of discussion about the nature and definition of giftedness and talent (see Gagné, 2004). One such discussion debates the relative value of potential ability versus its expression in the form of accomplishment.

The dust is far from settled in this debate and others like it, but it seems reasonable to assert that as exceptionally able children get older, the definitions of giftedness and talent shift from what students are capable of doing toward what they have actually done. In other words, young children may be considered gifted because they show great aptitude for certain areas, such as science. As children get older, what they actually have done—their talent—becomes a better indicator of what they may achieve next. For parents, this perspective highlights the importance of supporting and encouraging your child to apply her interests and abilities toward producing accomplishments in her field of interest.

Interest and its close relative, motivation, play a major role in the development of advanced ability. Studies of talent development have suggested that achieving eminence in any field of study requires at least 10,000 hours of dedicated study and practice (Bloom, 1985). However, young children often view talent development as play. Interest must come first, and interest and parental support together carry the child through the years of hard work that follow.

Set the Stage for Success

For very young children, everything is an attempt to solve problems or learn more about the world. Actions like opening and shaking "sippy cups," investigating what dog food tastes like, or thoroughly examining the contents of cupboards are all ways young children test their surroundings and learn about the world around them. Your reactions to their actions begin to shape their view of their surroundings. Promote safe exploration. Divert unacceptable actions rather than condemning them. Stay alert, aware, and encouraging.

For the somewhat older child, the questions change, but the intent remains the same. By the time a child is old enough to talk coherently, you can play thinking games that help encourage mental development. Games with many right answers, such as "Let's see how many things you can name that are furry," help children learn to produce many ideas. This ability, called *fluency*, is an important part of creative thinking. Such exercises also help the child develop connections between different things she knows, which is an important aspect of higher level thinking in many different areas.

Visualizing things in unusual ways, called *flexibility* in the creativity literature, is also a vital skill in many theoretical sciences. Well-known scientific advances, such as figuring out the structures of DNA and the benzene molecule, have resulted from an individual's ability to see things differently than everyone else. Play that draws on the child's imagination, such as making a cardboard box into a spaceship, can help develop this creative thinking ability. Some activities that develop flexibility can also help develop *elaboration*, which is the ability to add detail to ideas. More information on fluency, flexibility, and elaboration can be found in Table 6.

Help Your Child Master Process Skills

Science learning is different from learning in many other areas because it requires that learners master process skills (Ostlund, 1992). In one sense, process skills are closely related to the steps

Table 6 Three Key Scientific Skills You Can Help Your Child Develop		
Skill	Ability	Sample Word Game
Fluency	Develop connections	"How many things can you name that . . . ?"
Flexibility	See things in unusual ways	"How many things can we make with this?"
Elaboration	Add details to ideas	"How do you think the story should end?"

in the scientific method mentioned in Chapter 1. However, particularly at the basic level, process skills emphasize the individual hands-on skills needed to conduct scientific study, rather than scientific reasoning processes alone. Without the appropriate process skills such as the ability to make accurate and precise measurements of observations, researchers could not follow the scientific method. The chances for success in the science classroom, and later the laboratory, improve when your child enters the classroom already possessing these skills.

Various lists differ slightly, but the science process skills presented in Table 7 are generally thought to be central to success.

Many, if not all, of these process skills can be developed at home. Successfully teaching these skills requires a combination of explaining ideas, encouraging hands-on practice with objects, holding discussions, and providing feedback based on observations. This is, of course, how you as a parent already approach teaching anything else, from catching a baseball to gardening.

Table 7
Process Skills Needed for Success
in Hands-On Science

Basic Science Process Skills	Integrated Process Skills
Observing	Controlling variables
Inferring	Defining operationally
Measuring	Formulating hypotheses
Communicating	Interpreting data
Classifying	Experimenting
Predicting	Formulating models
Using numbers	Investigating
Using time/space relationships	Naming variables

Note. Compiled from Hershberger, 2000, and Padilla, 1990.

Even if you feel you are not comfortable teaching your child science, with some conscious effort you can apply these same instructional methods to teach your child process skills within any other field of learning.

There is nothing magic about teaching process skills. What makes this type of instruction effective is your conscious awareness of what you are doing and why. Share your own knowledge to help your child develop this type of awareness, known in education by the term *metacognition*. For example, explain to your child how his or her newly learned skills can and should be applied as needed to learning new material.

Many prominent scientists have or had parents who were not personally comfortable with science. However, these parents provided exceptional, supportive learning environments to their children. You can do the same.

Create a Supportive Learning Environment

As a parent interested in fully developing your child's potential, you should know about the work of the influential researcher, Benjamin Bloom, who died in 1999 at the age of 86. Over his long career, he strongly influenced all fields of education because—in good scientific research tradition—he amassed strong evidence from both the United States and abroad to support his hypothesis that early experiences in the home have a great impact on later learning, and that virtually all children can learn at a high level when appropriate practices are undertaken in the home and school. The theme throughout Bloom's work was that educational settings and home environments can foster human potential, a message that encouraged educational experiments and reform.

In the latter years of his career, Bloom turned his attention to talented youngsters, and led a research team that produced the book *Developing Talent in Young People,* published in 1985. Its message was that there is a broad group of people capable of achieving great talent, provided they receive the right experiences.

Bloom's studies (1985) offer specific guidance regarding features that make a particular home learning environment effective in promoting talent development. He described the most effective parents as "child-oriented and willing to devote their time, their resources, and their energy to giving each of their children the best conditions they could provide for them. Almost no sacrifice was too great" (p. 510).

This was far from being some sort of one-sided child worship, however. In the early years, these parents viewed their children's interests as ordinary, rather than extraordinary, even though their child's talents eventually did become quite extraordinary. The parents of successful children placed great emphasis on work ethic, on doing one's best at all times, and on achievement. Family activities emphasized the child's areas of interest (Sloane,

1985). However, when a child showed a particularly strong interest in an area, the factors these parents emphasized to their child were "to excel, to do one's best, to work hard, and to spend one's time constructively" (Bloom, 1985, p. 510). These effective parents expected their children to share in chores around the house and do them well. Family routines such as meals, recreation, and bedtimes were set up to give children appropriate responsibilities for their age and help them develop good self-discipline.

If you do not feel you are an expert in the field of your child's special gifts, take heart. Many of the parents in Bloom's study were not experts either, although many found themselves learning more as their children's talents developed in a particular field. In the early years of talent development, it is clearly expectations and the learning environment—rather than any special ability on the part of the parents—that makes the difference for talented children. The learning environment you create is more important than the particular games or activities you do with your child.

Five steps for an effective home learning environment include: devote time, energy, and resources to your child; emphasize work ethic; urge your child to do his best, work hard, and spend time constructively; give your child age-appropriate responsibilities; and establish family routines that foster self-discipline.

To encourage creative thinking, children, as well as adults, need to be able to take risks and make mistakes without fear of unduly harsh consequences. Children learn by asking questions about things that do not make sense to them. You can help your child develop scientific questioning skills by taking the time to answer such questions thoughtfully. Let your child know when a question has no answer. If you do not know the answer yourself, admit it rather than covering up the fact. Whenever possible, follow this admission by searching for the answer together. Sharing stories about your own experiences learning new things is yet another way of modeling learning behaviors for your child.

Encourage Individual Science Learning

A child who is unusually able in any way needs to be given the opportunity for a great deal of practice to move from merely bright to talented. For a young athlete, this may mean tiny golf clubs and the chance to follow her father around the golf course. For a musician, such as young Franz Schubert, it meant playing in a string quartet with his father and two brothers. For a young scientist, it means actually doing science.

> Allow your child to conduct supervised experiments at home.

Independent Investigations and Projects

Many prominent scientists recall conducting independent investigations and projects when they were young. At the age of 10, chemist Alan MacDiarmid worked his way through a book of chemistry experiments he found at the public library; for a year, he spent the money he earned from a paper route to buy the chemicals to do every experiment in this book. Many years later, in 2000, he shared the Nobel Prize in Chemistry for the discovery and development of conductive polymers (Hargittai, 2003).

Depending on where you live, your child's best opportunity to conduct similar activities may be at home. Due to insurance reasons and the fear of lawsuits, in some areas of the country even simple household chemicals such as sodium bicarbonate (baking soda) may not be used in schools. Certainly there are dangerous chemicals available even in the grocery store, but my personal reaction to this particular ban is that it is ridiculous. Baking soda is a major ingredient in many toothpaste formulations, and few if any people are injured putting these chemical mixtures in their mouth. Nevertheless, schools have to comply with these rules. Allowing your child to conduct experiments at home, under proper parental supervision and with proper attention to safety, can play an important part in developing his interests and abilities in science.

The Role of Puzzles and Toys

Puzzles and similar challenging toys can be quite useful in developing spatial ability and increasing students' interest and awareness of scientific phenomena. Educational organizations such as the National Association for Gifted Children annually publish lists of the year's best new educational toys, and these can be a helpful resource. Parents should also keep in mind the value of more traditional toys; Rubik's cube, the hit toy of the early 1980s, was developed in part to help students visualize three-dimensional spaces. Spatial ability is important in many areas of science and technology, and this relatively inexpensive toy may help children develop their spatial visualization skills.

> Encourage puzzles and games that develop spatial abilities.

Books in the *Teaching Science With Toys* series, such as *Teaching Physics With Toys* (Taylor, Poth, & Portman, 1995), are a good reference to have on hand, not only for toy possibilities, but also for ideas about what you and your child can do with these toys to promote science learning.

Plan Science-Based Family Recreation

Family trips and other science-based recreational activities offer a highly motivating way to encourage and nurture children's interest in science. Information about local attractions is usually available through a Chamber of Commerce or Visitor's Center, or by simply looking over the rack of brochures in the lobby of a nearby hotel. While your child is young, strive for exposure to the broad variety of careers and subject areas science encompasses. Encourage a broad curiosity toward scientific topics, while also giving lots of encouragement to specific interests as they emerge. As your child gets older and develops stronger interests in one or more particular subject areas, undertake activities designed with these areas in mind.

Family-based science encounters don't need to be expensive or elaborate. Recurring experiences are generally more effective than a series of once-in-a-lifetime trips. Complex, highly structured activities can be overwhelming for nearly all small children and many older folks, as well. A simpler trip, repeated frequently, is often a better choice.

> Repeat experiences whenever possible. Children will learn something new each time.

If you are fortunate enough to find a science museum or nature center nearby, these usually offer annual memberships at a reasonable rate. Children will want to visit the permanent museum exhibits repeatedly, and will learn something different with each visit. The temporary exhibits change over time and offer a new learning experience with each change. Most museums and nature centers offer talks by experts, as well as weekend and summer science activities for children. Museum membership benefits may also include a discount at the museum's gift shop, which can be a good source for locating science-related toys and games.

State and national parks and historic sites offer another source of opportunities to take part in science-based recreation. Interpreters regularly present educational programs to the public, and to support them, the parks often rely upon volunteer organizations in which children and parents can participate. Here, the point is less to learn about a specific technology or industry than it is to engage your child's interest. The interest generated by these and similar activities often can lead to the development of innovative science fair projects and other independent investigations in future years.

Strengthen Math and Language Skills

There is a reason why educators call mathematics and language the core of education; they form the center of almost every advanced endeavor. Strong math and language skills are highly correlated with the development of high levels of scientific ability. Do everything possible at home to encourage both.

Language skills are vital because scientific advances build upon what has come before. Particularly in high school and college, science courses cover a great deal of complex written material. Learning new vocabulary is vital to this process. Work with your child to keep up-to-date with these new terms. As with language learning, science builds later knowledge onto earlier learning. The student who falls behind in learning science vocabulary can have a difficult time catching up. At more advanced-level tasks such as writing reports for science fairs and laboratory classes, students' language skills are also vital to scientific communication.

> Many science classes require students to learn more new vocabulary each week than in a foreign language class.

Encouraging math and language skills can be an especially helpful approach to working with children who do not believe that science is enjoyable. Project-based learning and team competitions in particular (e.g., the Science Olympiad, Future Problem Solving, Academic Decathlon) tend to require a diverse array of skills. Encourage your child to work on projects or in groups that will take advantage of his or her particular interests, and he or she likely will become more comfortable with the science that goes along with them.

Capitalize on your child's language and literacy skills to encourage an interest in science (Smutny, Walker, & Meckstroth, 1997). Scientists are increasingly becoming aware of the importance of communicating their work effectively, and this awareness is affecting how science instruction in school is carried out (Thier & Daviss, 2002). Scientifically inclined students often have strong verbal skills, as well, so science instruction that emphasizes reading, writing, and other means of communication may be especially attractive to these children. You may wish to talk to your child's teacher about classroom activities that present scientific interests in these ways.

In many scientific disciplines, math skills are equally important. This is true not just in obvious fields like physics and physical chemistry; even disciplines such as ecology and psychology make use of sophisticated mathematical models and statistical analyses that require an understanding of calculus and other advanced mathematical coursework. Careers in engineering, computer science, metallurgy, or other applied or technological fields also require extensive training in high-level mathematical thinking.

Nurture Creative Abilities

Science is, at its heart, a very creative endeavor. In addition to language and math ability, scientists who do groundbreaking work also rely upon well-developed creative abilities. The life of the late Nobel Prize-winning physicist Richard P. Feynman offers a prominent example. In his fascinating 1985 autobiography *Surely You're Joking, Mr. Feynman*, several anecdotes demonstrate how his unique point of view proved useful in developing new solutions to problems in physics and other fields. Read it first for your own enjoyment, and then share it with any child old enough to appreciate it.

Creativity is a subject receiving escalating amounts of attention. Some sources of ideas for incorporating creative development in science, as well as other content areas include the books *Creativity in the Classroom: Schools of Curious Delight* (Starko, 2005), *Fostering Creativity in Gifted Students* (Cramond, 2005), and *Inventions and Inventing for Gifted Students* (Hébert, 2005).

Help Your Child Master Technology

Personal experience helps here, but even the most technologically illiterate parents can still encourage their child to master technological skills if they approach the subject correctly. It's important to do so sooner rather than later. Technology is often the great divider in our society today, separating young from old and haves from have-nots. Perhaps your child is already more computer-literate than you are. Certainly if your child is not already a technology expert, some of his or her classmates probably are.

Technology can be looked at in two ways in the context of science learning. The first concerns learning *about* technology, and the second concerns learning *using* technology. These two aspects are interrelated, because knowledge in both is vital to students' educational development.

You don't need to know it all yourself; you only need to demonstrate a willingness to learn alongside your child. Many children are good at understanding by analogy, and if interested, will persistently investigate a problem until they understand what is going on. Because career span is strongly related to productivity and eminence, an earlier start developing technology skills can provide quite a boost to your child's lifetime achievement.

Share Your Interest in the History of Science and Technology

The pace of change is rapid, and new advances depend on knowledge and understanding of earlier work. The audio CD, for example, probably could not have been developed without the tape recordings, records, and wax cylinders that came before it. Cell phones depend on our advanced understanding of both radio and telephone technology.

Historical accounts of technology development are usually interesting even to those who do not consider themselves scientifically inclined. Even if you haven't delved into this area before, do so for the sake of being a strong role model. Expect to be more interested than you thought you'd be.

Read with your child about the history of technology. Excellent books abound, as do magazines such as *American Heritage of Invention and Technology*, a magazine sponsored by General Motors, but refreshingly restrained in advertising material. Watch technology-related programs on the History Channel. Bring home DVDs of both good and bad movies that feature science and technology; discuss them with your child as you watch them and afterward. Subscribe to the weekly journal, *Science News,* which features short digests of current topics in science, math, and technology, or other science and technology related periodicals.

Start now—time is working against you. As science fiction writer Arthur C. Clarke famously observed in the early 1960s, "any sufficiently advanced technology is indistinguishable from magic." Anyone could look carefully at a gramophone and a record with a magnifying glass and figure out how it works, with little scientific background needed to figure out the system. The same cannot be said of a CD and CD player. With every year that goes by, more and more background must be understood before one can proceed to the next level of technology. (This explosion of knowledge also helps to explain why most scientific advances are now made by teams, rather than by individual inventors.)

Guide Your Child in the Proper Use of Technology

The use of technology as a learning aid is advancing rapidly, and helps make up for the increased content children must master. Word processors allow us to make changes without having to retype entire pages, as was once required on a typewriter. Calculators with the power of a hand-held computer cut out the tedious work of higher level mathematical problems.

Google™ and similar search engines are one of the engineering wonders of the modern world—anyone with an Internet connection has access to more than 8 billion Web pages worldwide with just a few keystrokes. Students are gradually becoming more sophisticated about using information gathered from the Internet as these skills filter into the school curriculum, but for many students, the Internet is still the equivalent of a big encyclopedia. Copying material verbatim from the Web is even easier than copying from the encyclopedia was for the students of an earlier generation.

Similarly, temptations abound to use the Internet in inappropriate or illegal ways. For a technologically talented child, in particular, it can seem incredibly easy to pirate music, movies, and other material. Breaking into sites and files can seem like a challenge or a harmless game. As one parent said, "I never told him not to do it, because it never occurred to me that he would or could."

We all want to trust our children, but this is not the time to bury one's head in the sand. Talk to your child about proper use of this powerful resource. Stay involved. Read the papers they are turning in at school. You should and must help your child learn not only how to use the Internet, but how to use it critically and honestly. Online resources are available on this topic, and school media specialists and public and university libraries may also offer classes on using the Internet effectively.

Taking Advantage of Community Resources

Achievement begins at home, as you and your young child work and play together, beginning to develop his or her physical and social skills in preparation for adulthood. However, as your child grows, his or her interests begin to turn outside the family circle. Role models, mentors, peers, and community interests become increasingly important influences on your child. As an involved parent, you'll want to ensure that these influences are positive ones.

Help Your Child Find Others With Similar Interests

Particularly during the preteen and teenage years, it can be very important to children to associate with a group of people of similar age, background, and interests. Finding a peer group can be a challenge for the scientifically advanced child, particularly if he or she is somewhat of a loner by nature. Be as creative as possible in helping your child find a socially acceptable niche. School clubs, 4-H, scouting programs, and other such groups are worth checking into; for additional ideas see the appendix to this book.

Neighborhood or community groups may also provide leads to groups of adults in particular fields of interest. Such sources may range from Audubon Society chapters for the child deeply interested in birds, to aviation clubs at a local airport for the aeronautically inspired. Although you may have to accompany a child who is younger than 18 to meetings and activities, such groups may be appropriate for any child old enough to have the necessary attention span. They provide the opportunity to develop specialized skills in a field, and are particularly important for children whose interests lie outside of the regular school curriculum. As students grow older, such groups may also provide opportunities to gain leadership experience, benefiting students directly, as well as helping them gain admission to college.

Older siblings, cousins, or children of your friends can be particularly effective role models, but be careful to emphasize to your child that his or her interests will probably be quite different; the emphasis should be placed on the processes through which the older child's achievements were made, and not on repeating the exact path that was taken. It can also be effective to ask the older child, in private, to encourage your child. Emphasizing the importance of hard work is particularly important, because research suggests that children are more likely to achieve if they perceive their abilities as talents developed through their own sustained effort rather than as innate gifts.

Match Your Child With an Enrichment Program

Within many communities and across the nation, programs for scientifically advanced children abound. Many are excellent, but choose carefully. Consider the program's cost, location, and schedule. Bear in mind your child's age and social and emotional needs, as well as academic ones. One child might learn most effectively at a summer-camp program that offers a strong hands-on component and ample social activities. Another child may be better suited to a Saturday program at the science department of a nearby university.

Consider the potential peer group, as well. Some programs have a selective admissions process based on test scores or similar criteria, while others are available to any child whose parents can afford to pay. If your child does not have a strong peer group at school, a program catering primarily to children with similar interests and abilities may be an appropriate choice. If money is an issue in your home, your child may feel out of place in a nonexclusive, but expensive program. Always ask about the possibility of financial aid if you think you may qualify; it may be available yet not well-publicized.

As your child matures, your role in this decision should move increasingly in the direction of guidance only. Older children in particular should be granted considerable input into the selection of enrichment opportunities. Experience making choices at this stage will serve as good preparation for selecting an undergraduate or graduate school a few years later in life.

Find Your Child a Mentor

Mentoring is the process in which a less experienced person works individually under the guidance of a more experienced one. It can be one of the more effective learning methods available (Davalos & Haensly, 1997; Passow, 1988; Siegel & Shaughnessy, 1991). Because mentoring relationships typically focus on passing on skills and insider knowledge within a particular field of study, they are most appropriate for meeting the learning needs of older students who already have strong knowledge of a field's factual content.

Teachers can be excellent mentors, particularly if they are retired and therefore have schedules somewhat more forgiving than teachers who are in the classroom most of the day. College professors, whether retired or not, may also be an excellent source of this type of help. An advantage of both is that in addition to being quite experienced, they enjoy helping students learn.

Colleges and universities may also be a useful source of mentors, particularly through formal programs such as Big Brothers Big Sisters and other similar programs. Keep in mind, however, that a mentor is not the same as a tutor. Generally speaking, mentors work with their protégés voluntarily to develop skills and knowledge in a broad sense, while tutors are paid to work on specific academic skills. Tutors can also be a tremendous resource for developing your child's academic ability, especially once your child grows academically beyond your level of knowledge in a subject.

If you are fortunate enough to have friends who are scientific professionals, these individuals may also be willing to introduce your child to their work and describe how they prepared themselves for it. Talk with such contacts beforehand to be sure they emphasize to your child the rewards, as well as the hard work that are a part of such careers.

Mentoring is such an important topic that we'll return to it in the particular context of maintaining girls' interests in math, science, and technology.

Keeping Your Daughter in the Science Pipeline

The good news is that science today tends to be a fairly egalitarian field of study. The bad news is that, while there is no logical reason for your girl to feel her sex is inferior to that of boys, when it comes to math, science, and technology, virtually all girls are at risk for bypassing those fields for others. In the early elementary years, girls and boys do equally well on tests and grades in math, science, and technology. However, as female students progress through school and into college and graduate school, despite their frequently higher course grades, the top range of girls score lower on standardized tests than the top range of boys do. Girls take fewer advanced courses, and they drop out of these fields earlier than males do.

In their 1991 report *Shortchanging Girls, Shortchanging America*, the American Association of University Women (AAUW) identified the relationship between confidence and educational opportunities as critical to girls' success, particularly in science and math. They noted that schools unintentionally cheat girls of classroom attention by stressing competitive rather than cooperative learning, by presenting texts and lessons devoid of women as role models, and by reinforcing negative stereotypes about girls' abilities. Unconsciously, teachers and school counselors also often dampen girls' aspirations, particularly in math and science. In the ensuing years since this report there have been efforts to correct the situation, but there still are nowhere near enough gender equity programs in science, math, and technology (AAUW, 1998; Campbell & Clewell, 1999).

As adults, females are underrepresented in most scientific fields. Recent studies have found that among college-bound high school seniors, females are three to four times less likely to have pursued a degree in physical science, computer science, mathematics, or engineering, while young women outnumber young men only in the biological sciences and health profession majors (Joyce & Faregna, 2000). The fact that there are, on average, more female than male students actually attending college makes these differences stand out even more strongly.

Patterns of gender differences in scientific interests appear to begin as early as primary school and continue through adulthood. A variety of causes have been suggested, but it appears that social and cultural expectations share much of the responsibility for these differences. Keeping your daughter in the "science pipeline" as she matures can be a challenge if she feels isolated or strange by virtue of being a female interested in science. An appropriate home environment, peer groups, and mentoring can all help counteract this feeling.

Science Success for Girls Begins at Home

Make sure that your children's activities are not automatically divided along gender lines. Think carefully about the toys you give your children—these provide a major, yet frequently overlooked, source of their ideas about the world. If you have children of both sexes, make sure you give science toys to both and not just to the boy(s) in the house.

Talk to your children often about women in science. If your children pick up stereotypes about science careers from friends or at school, offer contrasting examples. For example, if your daughter tells you that "all scientists are old men in white coats," point out that her aunt Emily is a scientist, but is not old, or a man, even though she may wear a white lab coat at work.

Keep up the encouragement and support as your daughter matures. The interests and abilities in science that you foster in your daughter can have wider ramifications than most people realize. The AAUW study on American girls' education (1991) found a strong relationship between perceived math and science skills and adolescent self-esteem. Of all the study's indicators, girls' perceptions of their ability in math and science had the strongest relationship to their self-esteem. As girls "learned" that they were not good at these subjects, their sense of self-worth and aspirations for themselves deteriorated.

As long as her home makes up her whole world, your daughter is likely to feel that she is an equally valuable human being. However, as she gets older she may begin to notice that in the world outside the home, women are often treated as a minority group. In the turbulent years of early adolescence, her school age-mates often become an additional source of tension and disapproval.

There seem to be two ways people may react when faced with trouble. Some people react by becoming kinder and nobler; other become more disorganized, emotionally upset, and destructive. Psychological tests seem to indicate that these reaction types may also characterize women reacting to discrimination against them. How can you prepare your daughter to react constructively and without bitterness? A happy and beloved childhood, starting early and lasting long, is a good start. The attitude of a little girl's father makes a lot of difference. Watching to see how he treats other women in the family gives a daughter an indication of where she herself stands. Equally, girls learn early how their mothers feel about being a woman, how they react to adversity, and how they solve problems. The feelings and strategies of women are contagious, and can be passed on from generation to generation. The best way to help a daughter have a constructive attitude is to have one yourself.

> Prepare your daughter for obstacles in such a way that she will react constructively rather than with bitterness.

Help Your Daughter Find a Science-Related Peer Group of Females

During the preteen and teenage years, children desire to associate with a group of people of similar age, background, and interests. Nationwide groups such as the Canadian Association for Girls in Science and the Sally Ride Science Club™ in the United States (see appendix for more information) offer newsletters, information, and online discussion groups to promote girls' interests in science. The Girl Scouts of America has recently launched the "Girls Go Tech" initiative to promote math, science, and technology learning for girls. See http://www.girlsgotech. org/index.html for more information and a downloadable brochure with activity ideas and tips for parents. Prominent universities such as Vanderbilt and Columbia have offered weekend and summer programs designed specifically for girls to encourage them to pursue interests in technology, math, science, and engineering. Locally sponsored science programs for girls often are administered by museums, community organizations, and nonprofit foundations.

> A peer group will let your daughter explore and develop her interests in science and related areas with other girls.

There are hundreds of these programs across the country. Because direct personal contact is best, start your search locally. Consult with organizations in your local area to find out what programs or clubs may be available to your child. Then go online; the suggestions in the appendix of this book provide a good jumping-off place. Table 8 provides more suggestions for increasing your daughter's success in science and technology fields.

Find a Mentor for Your Daughter

How can you encourage your daughter to achieve in science? For older students, mentoring is particularly effective, especially when the mentor is sensitive to the needs of young women entering a male-dominated field of study (Siegel & Shaughnessy, 1991;

Table 8
Eight Ways to Increase Your Daughter's Success in Science and Technology

---

1. Engage her by encouraging collaboration and cooperation.

2. Help her find peers who support and share her interests.

3. Encourage her to use her computer skills to be creative and customize her learning.

4. Help her connect to female role models who exemplify real situations and career paths.

5. Teach her new skills that are applicable to girls' interests.

6. Provide ways for her to demonstrate or teach her skills to others.

7. Teach her positive ways to react to obstacles.

8. Expect success and achievement.

Subotnik & Arnold, 1995). In fact, such mentoring may almost be essential. In a study following up on Westinghouse Science Talent Search winners, poor or nonexistent mentoring actually led some of these scientifically gifted young women to abandon their career aspirations in math or science (Subotnik, Stone, & Steiner, 2001). On the other hand, mentoring programs such as CyberSisters, which hosts an online public mentoring program at its Web site (http://www.cyber-sisters.org) have had a remarkable influence on girls' success.

What makes a girl's mentoring effective? Apparently the same approaches that work for boys (e.g., see Davalos & Haensly,

1997). Refer back to the earlier section on mentoring for more on this. Keep in mind that many students and mentors may feel most comfortable working with others of the same ethnicity and gender, so mentoring relationships should be set up to allow such matching whenever possible. Finding an ideal mentoring match may pose an added difficulty for girls, and particularly for minority girls, as the majority of scientists remain nonminority and male. Nevertheless, because mentoring has played such an important role in the lives of so many successful female scientists, it is to your daughter's advantage if you can work with her to develop these types of relationships.

Chapter 4

School Experiences: Being Your Child's Best Advocate

T he family is the basic unit of society, but in a highly organized society like ours, community life is also tremendously important. As your child gets older, your community and society at large will influence your child more strongly and more directly. How can you make this interaction between your child and the outside world as constructive as possible?

School provides the most important set of experiences your child has away from home. Here he or she learns not only basic living tools such as reading, mathematics, and science, but also basic training in attitudes and work habits that may last a lifetime.

Unfortunately, research has firmly established that interest in science generally drops as children progress through school (Simpson & Oliver, 1985), and this drop is particularly dramatic during the middle and high school years. It doesn't need to be this way. Your knowledge and a friendly, positive interest in your child's school can make a difference.

This chapter offers advice, based on relevant research and experience, about how to work effectively with schools to ensure that your child's educational needs are met, particularly in the area of science. Although each individual situation is different, the general approaches presented here have been effective in a wide variety of circumstances. If you have tried each of these approaches and have been unsuccessful, Chapter 5 presents some alternatives to traditional schooling.

What to Expect From the Typical K–12 School Curriculum

The typical public school curriculum is quite limited in the scope of science courses it offers to students, and this is another reason why parents often must take the initiative in offering science enrichment to their scientifically talented child.

Primary and Elementary School

Typically, the elementary science curriculum focuses on the study of the environment—an appropriate, readily accessible area of study for young children. Many schools use vegetable gardens, butterfly gardens, nature trails, and similar outdoor activities to develop student interest; schools in more urban settings often keep fish tanks, terrariums, and other microhabitats to expose children to science. However, the development and use of these resources is quite dependent on the individual teacher. Within a single school, some teachers may incorporate scientific learning consistently, while other teachers hardly use the available resources at all.

Furthermore, some schools integrate science activities into language arts or social studies curricula rather than giving them a dedicated time in the school day. In some cases, the lack of a dedicated time can lead to inadequate coverage of science topics. In other cases, state standards may mandate such treatment, particularly when test scores in English and math are strongly emphasized. There is wide variation in the quality and quantity of elementary science instruction, and many teachers at this level seem to feel uncomfortable teaching scientific topics. You may need to discuss these issues with local school personnel to determine the most suitable placement for your child. Table 9 discusses some positive steps you can take to resolve some of the issues you may face regarding your child's science education in elementary school.

Middle School/Junior High School

Schools generally group students into either middle schools (usually grades 6–8) or junior high schools (often grades 7–9). Although these terms have some implications for how a school is structured, for this book I have used the term *middle school* to refer collectively to all students in these grade ranges.

Middle school science curricula vary widely, but generally include the equivalent of one year of life science (biology), one year of earth science (primarily geology), and one year of physical science (a combination of physics and chemistry). Some middle school curricula present each of these subjects sequentially.

Table 9 **Issues With Science Education in Elementary** **School and Ways to Resolve Them**	
Potential Pitfalls in Elementary School	Positive Steps You Can Take
Limited science offerings or no science instruction at all.	• Find avenues for out-of-school science enrichment for your child. • Volunteer to come into the class- room on a regular basis to offer special programs to the whole class. • Start an after-school science club. • Work to bring groups such as 4-H into the school.
Teachers differ in the amount of science they offer.	• Talk with teachers, administrators, and other parents to determine the most suitable placement for your child. • Talk directly to the teacher in a friendly, positive manner to find ways to provide support.

Others use a spiral approach, teaching similar material drawn from all three fields in a continuous, integrated fashion while going into greater depth about the fields during each successive year.

At the middle school level, students generally encounter a full-time science teacher for the first time. This can be a critical juncture in terms of awakening or killing a child's interest in science. Young people of this age are often critical, quickly judge adults, and are prone to equate a subject with the teacher who presents it.

For the advanced student, this teacher can present a valuable resource, being an admired person in authority who can answer most of the student's persistent questions about scientific topics. However, if the science teacher is poorly prepared, careless, or frequently makes mistakes in class, problems may arise. The able student at this age will readily pick up on factual errors, but may not yet have developed the social skills to point out the teacher's error in a tactful manner. In response, some teachers may become defensive, antagonistic, or passive-aggressive toward bright students. Do your homework; talk to other parents. Take the time to ensure that your child is assigned to a teacher worthy of becoming an inspiration and continuing mentor. Table 10, and the following paragraphs, presents some of the other problems children may face in their science education in middle school, and positive steps parents can take to overcome these problems.

Peer pressure against science interests, particularly for girls, also comes into play especially strongly at this age (Talton & Simpson, 1985). For many children, science comes to be seen as something elitist, difficult, and exclusionary; in response, it is shunned, and sometimes those children who continue to display an interest in science are rejected or ignored by their classmates. As a parent, you can help by being proactive. Even before your child reaches middle school, help him or her develop a wide circle of friendships with others who are like-minded and scientifically inclined.

Recognize that the science offerings at your child's school may have been implemented in response to the requirements of standardized testing. In accordance with the No Child Left Behind Act of 2001 (NCLB), beginning in 2007, all states must test student science achievement every year, and must test students at least once in grades 3–5, 6–9, and 10–12.

Table 10 **Problems Your Child May Face in Middle School Science**	
Potential Pitfalls in Middle School	Positive Steps You Can Take
Peer pressure to abandon science.	Be proactive; involve your child with a science-oriented peer group.
Child's judgment of teacher may influence his or her judgment on science.	Do your homework; match your child to a good teacher.
Textbook errors.	Help your child write a letter to the publisher.
Science class may be all paper, pencil, and textbook.	Do every positive, constructive thing you can do to help the teacher and school implement hands-on science activities, both in class and in extracurricular activities.

An unfortunate consequence is that teachers may use these tests—and administrative pressure arising from them—as excuses to base their instruction entirely on textbooks, disregarding long-known and well-documented research (e.g., see Bybee & Sund, 1990; Inhelder & Piaget, 1958) that indicates that most children of this age are able to think hypothetically only when given concrete examples. Many teachers shun inquiry-based instruction because they are uncomfortable with activities that may not have predictable results. Likewise, they hesitate to venture outside the classroom; in various surveys more than 80% of seventh and eighth graders have reported never going on field trips with their science classes. (This problem is not a new one; unfortunately, if anything, the numbers are substantially higher in today's climate of shrinking budgets and escalating liability lawsuits plaguing schools. For an example of one such survey, see Mullis & Jenkins, 1988.)

An additional problem with this reliance on textbook-based instruction is that many of the science textbooks schools use are poorly written or even incorrect. A study conducted by the American Association for the Advancement of Science (Roseman, Kesidou, Stern, & Caldwell, 1999) found that none of the middle grade science texts they reviewed were adequate. Most middle school science texts cover too much material in too little depth, the study concluded, inadvertently introducing errors by covering topics too briefly and superficially. Worse, the texts often feature classroom activities that are not particularly relevant or helpful for teaching students about the underlying scientific ideas they are trying to learn (Hubisz, 2003).

Although there have been some improvements since these studies were conducted, the textbook replacement cycle is long, and some schools still may be using these poor materials. As a result, students may learn material that is incorrect, or not learn what they are supposed to know. If you as a parent or your child's older siblings have any scientific background at all, you can help your child immensely by being particularly attentive to the science learning of children during the middle grades.

What should you do if you find errors or problems? Your first inclination, and probably that of your scientifically advanced child, as well, may be to point out these errors to the teacher. Although a good teacher will recognize the limitations of any textbook and will turn errors in the book into an opportunity for student learning, not all teachers will possess these skills. Some teachers may view you as a troublemaker and/or your child's quest for truth as disrespectful toward their authority, with negative consequences for your child.

Consider other alternatives, such as turning this into an opportunity for your child to correspond with the textbook publisher. Help him or her write an effective letter, documenting the reasons why the textbook material seems incomplete, misleading, or inaccurate. Most people are unaware that publishers usually will take such correspondence quite seriously, and forward it to the book authors for comment, then respond to the letter writer. In other cases, a publisher will not reply directly, but still take action to correct the error in the next edition. Remind your child that the response may take a while to arrive, because it travels through several channels.

By taking this route, you've not only averted a possible confrontation between your child and the teacher, but you've turned the experience into a valuable lesson on effective communication and appropriate positive action for change. Instead of focusing on the teacher and the error, your child is encouraged to focus on the altruistic motive of helping publishers—who, after all, have done their best with a very intricate job—to present the correct information to other students in the future.

High School

High school is in many ways just a ratcheted-up version of middle school, and in fact some school systems still combine junior and senior high schools into a single entity. Though the students may be slightly more mature, they face essentially the same pitfalls as they did in middle school, with a few more added on top.

At the high school level, usually grades 9–12, science courses in the curriculum expand, but to a degree that seems to depend largely on school size. In smaller high schools and in rural areas, choices such as distance learning may provide the only options for study beyond a limited handful of in-school courses. Teachers in these settings may be required to teach several different courses at once, or even teach courses outside their areas of expertise or certification. Table 11 presents some of the additional problems students face in their high school science education.

Larger schools usually offer a wider variety of science classes, giving students greater opportunities to pursue their individual interests in particular fields of study. Core courses such as physical science, biology, and chemistry are usually available at two or even three levels of difficulty, depending on school and community needs. Physics, ecology, and human anatomy may be available to advanced students. Many top students may take two or three science classes each year, graduating with seven or more science courses on their transcript. Advanced Placement classes (see below) are increasingly common, offering students the chance to do accelerated work and receive college credit if their final examination scores in the subject are high enough.

Still, science is a huge field of endeavor, and dozens of scientific disciplines are rarely if ever made available to students. The highly able student whose interests lie in entomology, hydrology, or archaeology would hardly be aware that these fields exist if he were limited to the content of the school science curriculum. Some enlightened schools will allow a student to work independently with an interested teacher to pursue such interests; others may allow joint enrollment with a nearby college or university. However, many highly able students may not be able to pursue either of these possibilities. In these cases, options such as distance learning and special summer programs can be just what the student needs to round out the coursework available in school. These possibilities are discussed in further detail later in this book.

Table 11 Problems Students Face in Their High School Science Education	
Potential Pitfalls in High School	Positive Steps You Can Take
The same pitfalls as in middle school may appear for the first time or intensify.	• Be proactive; begin or continue the actions recommended for the middle school years.
Many science courses are offered, but none are in the specialized areas that most interest your child.	• Help your student pursue options such as independent study, distance learning, and summer programs.
Some schools make Advanced Placement courses available to students; others don't.	• Inquire about prerequisites early. • Check all local high schools. • Consider independent study for the AP exam.

The Advanced Placement Program

Advanced Placement (AP) courses originally were designed several decades ago to make college-level coursework available to the most able high school students. In recent years, AP course enrollment nationwide has risen dramatically. Today more schools offer these courses than ever before, and increasing numbers of students in each school take advantage of the opportunity AP classes present. At the end of a year of intensive study, AP students pay a fee for the opportunity to take a nationally administered exam in the subject. Students making scores of 3, 4, or 5 on the tests' five-point scale can receive college credit for a semester or even a year of introductory coursework, depending on their score, the subject, and the particular university's policies.

Parents generally like the AP program. Unlike options such as dual enrollment, AP courses place students with others of similar age and maturity, and do not require students to leave the high school campus. Furthermore, AP courses are offered within the regular school and generally on the regular school schedule. The AP examination fees are sometimes paid by the school or district to encourage all qualified students to take the exams. However, even if parents have to pay these fees out of pocket, the cost is much less than the tuition costs students would otherwise pay in college for an equivalent number of credits.

As the AP program has grown, having taken AP classes has become increasingly important in college admission. Nearly all applicants to competitive universities will have been successful in several AP courses. Because Advanced Placement classes are much more rigorous than regular high school classes, a B grade in an AP class is often weighted to be equivalent to an A in a regular course when schools calculate student grade point averages.

Students usually take Advanced Placement classes in grades 10–12, although some exceptional students have been successful as early as the eighth grade. Some schools make AP classes available to all interested students. Others have established prerequisites, such as having achieved an A or B in a previous advanced science class. Check with your child's school well ahead of time to be aware of what its requirements are.

If your child is interested in a science field that has no corresponding AP course at your high school, do a little investigation. Sometimes different high schools within a district may offer different AP courses. It may be possible to arrange transportation to another school to take the course there. Alternatively, independent study may be possible. The Advanced Placement program allows students to pay the fee and take the course examination even without enrollment in a formal AP class.

Timing Coursework for Success

Does it seem likely that your child will be a candidate for advanced work in high school? Get ready early, because improper timing of prerequisites can trip up these plans. For the scientifically inclined student, two courses are particularly apt to cause problems—algebra and biology.

Getting into the top tier of high school classes often requires that a student has successfully completed Algebra I in the eighth grade—one year ahead of the usual schedule. In many schools, Algebra I is a prerequisite for advanced physical science, which is in turn a prerequisite for advanced chemistry. For example, in the school where I taught, advanced students took physical science as 9th graders, then biology, then advanced chemistry as 11th graders. Advanced Placement chemistry was only available to students who had already completed advanced chemistry, which meant that most students could only take this class in their final year of high school. Students who had taken regular rather than advanced physical science were strongly discouraged from enrolling in advanced chemistry, and the average-level chemistry course was not accepted as a prerequisite for the AP chemistry course. To complicate matters further, the school labeled all of these courses "college preparatory," a practice that could trip up students and parents who may be unaware of the differences between the two levels. Advanced Placement classes in physics and calculus (both of which may be available as 2-year sequences, as well) operate in a similar manner and also depend heavily on the completion of Algebra I in the eighth grade.

Some schools, however, do not offer algebra to eighth graders. A helpful alternative in this case is to swap the student's enrollment in the sciences, so he or she takes biology in the ninth grade and defers physical science until tenth grade. This will allow your child an additional year to refine mathematical reasoning skills and complete Algebra I before enrolling in the math-intensive physical sciences classes. Another potential option for the qualified student is to take Algebra I as a summer course; if your school or another does not offer it locally, look for it as a widely available offering through the regional talent search programs.

How Curriculum Is Shaped: The Science Standards

Two nationally recognized science standards outline what educators believe students should know, understand, and be able to do in the sciences over the course of a public school education.

Although these two sets of standards were developed as separate initiatives, they share about 90% of their content in common. The Project 2061 standards are more comprehensive and have more supporting material available in the form of printed materials, online resources, and professional development opportunities for teachers. At present, most state science learning standards have some basis in these standards, as well.

Project 2061

The American Association for the Advancement of Science (AAAS) has developed the Project 2061 standards, named for the year that Comet Halley will next return to Earth. These standards have been in existence since 1989. New supporting programs and materials are added regularly, including *Science for All Americans* (Rutherford & Ahlgren, 1990), *Benchmarks for Science Literacy* (AAAS, 1993), and *The Dialogue on Early Childhood Science, Mathematics, and Technology Education* (AAAS, 1999). These and other related resources are available both in print and online (http://www.project2061.org/publications/toolWeb.htm) as searchable documents; they are also available in Spanish.

The organization of the Project 2061 standards is presented in *Science for All Americans.* Taken as a whole, the book effectively describes what scientific literacy looks like. The companion volume, *Benchmarks for Science Literacy*, specifies how students can progress toward achieving this goal, including what students should know and be capable of doing when they have completed so-called benchmark grade levels (2, 5, 8, and 12). More recently, *Designs for Science Literacy* (AAAS, 2001) offers guidance to teachers and others who are developing science curricula.

National Science Education Standards

The other relevant set of standards is the *National Science Education Standards,* published by the National Academy of Sciences in 1996, and available now online (http://books.nap.edu/html/nses/html/overview.html#content). Hundreds of people, from teachers and parents to scientists, engineers, and government officials, cooperated to develop the NSES. Major corporations, foundations, and organizations joined in a massive effort to combine the results of research, earlier reform efforts, and personal insights to produce a broad consensus about the elements of science education they believed would permit all students to achieve their scientific potential. Table 12 provides a list of some of these elements NSES encourages students to learn.

Table 12
Categories of Study in the National Science Education Standards

NSES categories include:
- unifying concepts and processes in science,
- science as inquiry,
- physical science,
- life science,
- earth and space science,
- science and technology,
- science in personal and social perspective, and
- history and nature of science.

These standards continue to influence and guide U.S. science education, and have encouraged many states to mount similar efforts. Organized within eight categories, they address content that should be understood or abilities that should be developed through science instruction in grades K–4, 5–8, and 9–12.

Use Science Standards to Advocate for Your Child at School

As the parent of a scientifically talented child, you will want to make the effort to become familiar with national science standards. The Project 2061 materials are extensive, yet are not difficult reading. Read *Science for All Americans* to familiarize yourself with the overall goals that your child should strive toward in math, science, and technology learning. However, the *Benchmarks* volume may be more useful in helping you to evaluate your child's current status and the yearly progress he or she is making toward these learning goals.

Your child's science teacher, science department head, or other school administrator should be able to discuss the Project 2061 materials with you, and should be able to explain to your satisfaction how these standards and goals inform the classroom instruction your child receives. These materials have been used in science teacher preparation programs for many years, and they represent up-to-date thinking about what effective science instruction should look like. If it does not appear that your child's teacher is aware of these resources, you will want to find out why.

Keep in mind that the *Benchmarks* book is not intended to serve as a curriculum; rather, they describe the outcomes that locally selected science curricula should produce. In fact, the *Benchmarks* book is designed to allow and even lead toward a greater diversity of science curricula than currently are used in teaching science. *Designs for Science Literacy* is intended to offer guidance in curriculum development, but this book also does not prescribe any particular approach. This distinction is quite important—Project 2061's support for the use of a variety of curricula can lend support in advocating for appropriately differentiated curriculum and instruction for children.

> **Content** is what students should learn. **Curriculum** is the way content is presented, organized, and emphasized.

Use Standards to Guide Science Learning at Home

In addition to their impact on what your child learns in school, you may wish to use the Project 2061 guidelines to direct your child's learning at home, supplementing or even replacing the education received in school (see the section on homeschooling in Chapter 5). The AAAS materials suggest general directions in which to extend students' science learning. The *Benchmarks* book classifies concepts by general topic (e.g., "Processes That Shape the Earth"), and further divide these into grade range categories (such as grades 3–5). At this level, *Benchmarks* suggests, students may "build devices for demonstrating how wind and water shape the land and how forces on materials can make wrinkles, folds, and faults" (p. 72).

Project 2061 emphasizes that deeper understanding of a few topics is more useful than superficial knowledge of a great many.

If your child does not seem to be doing activities like this in school, you may wish to look into some of the many science curriculum Web sites online to find activities in these areas to conduct with your child at home. Be aware that the *Benchmarks* book describes a minimum level of knowledge, not a maximum. These standards should be used as a starting point for extending learning in whatever additional directions interest the child.

Over the past several decades, the depth of science instruction has suffered as public school science textbooks have added more and more breadth of material. More material means that there is less opportunity to examine any particular issue in detail. This trend may hold especially true for students with some prior knowledge of a science subject, because a common classroom response to students who finish quickly is simply to give them more of the same until the rest of the class has caught up. Breadth of knowledge is important, but it is becoming increasingly evident that a deep understanding of a few issues may be more useful in the long run than a superficial knowledge of many. Long-term independent projects and competitions (see Chapter 6) and other classroom-based activities can offer a variety of effective alternatives to providing additional worksheets or other superficial activities.

Navigating the School System in Support of Your Scientifically Inclined Child

Despite the slightly hysterical tone that pervades the popular press, schools generally do a good to adequate job for most average-ability students. However, they are often less successful with those students at the far ends of the ability range.

Parents of children with unusual gifts often report that interactions with the school system are a source of frustration in their lives. Prominent reports such as *A Nation Deceived: How Schools Hold Back America's Brightest Students* (Colangelo, Assouline, & Gross, 2004) and others (Delisle, 2003) illustrate the source of much of this tension—many schools do not do a good job of educating their best and brightest students. The situation appears to have worsened with recent trends that favor placing students of all ability levels within the same classroom. Teachers with appropriate training can still provide for the varied needs that result from these mixed ability classes (Johnsen, Haensly, Ryser, & Ford, 2002), but such training may not be readily available in every area.

Understand the Educational Rights of Your Child

As a scientifically talented student, your child can seem to be in a strange educational limbo. You routinely find that some of the politicians and administrators who hold power over educational decisions affecting your child act as though special talents are such an advantage that no concessions are needed. Others view the talented child as one who doesn't fit into the mainstream and is therefore analogous to (and sometimes lumped in with) the child with physical or mental disabilities. This viewpoint underlies the preemption of the word *exceptional*, which was once used to mean outstanding, but is now routinely applied to those who have disabilities.

If one holds the latter view, it is worth being aware that all students with disabilities are guaranteed a free and appropriate public education under the terms of several federal laws. These laws include the Individuals with Disabilities Educational Act (IDEA), Section 504 of the Rehabilitation Act of 1973, Americans with Disabilities Act (ADA), and most recently, the Family Educational Right to Privacy Act (FERPA).

The federal government appears to support the idea of special services for students with unusual abilities. Federal regulations describe gifted students as those that:

> ... perform or show the potential for performing at remarkably high levels of accomplishment when compared with others of their age, experience, or environment. These children and youth exhibit high performance capability in intellectual, creative, and/or artistic areas, possess an unusual leadership capacity, or excel in specific academic fields. They require services or activities not ordinarily provided by the schools. (U.S. Department of Education, 1993, p. 26)

But, while this definition states that these students "require services," federal regulations stop short of mandating that schools provide such services to these bright children. State-level regulations therefore bear the responsibility for supporting or ignoring the needs of these students. Because appropriate services cost money, only a handful of states have adopted legislation that both mandates gifted education services and funds them adequately.

Even if your child is not served in a gifted program, you should make every effort to familiarize yourself with the regulations in your state. State gifted associations usually publicize this information, and state departments of education will also present this information on their Web sites. A list of state gifted associations is available online from the National Association for Gifted Children (see http://www.nagc.org). A comparative list of state policies, maintained by the Davidson Institute for Talent Development, is also available online (see http://www. geniusdenied.com/Policies/StatePolicy.aspx).

Develop a Good Relationship With Teachers and Administrators

Among school personnel, involved parents often have a reputation as pushy or worse. Unfortunately, this perception often has its roots in teachers' personal experiences. Do your best to counteract this negative stereotype.

Do everything you can to develop a good relationship with your child's teachers and school administrators (Hertzog, 2003). If your other responsibilities permit it, spend time volunteering at your child's school. There is a strong correlation between the time parents spend in schools and overall student achievement, so your assistance may improve the overall educational experience at the school, while also developing a positive relationship between you and the school personnel who work with your child.

Researcher Karen Rogers (2005) studied the factors that led to a successful implementation of individualized education plans for highly able students. She found that only about one in five families were successful in obtaining an individualized education plan for their high-ability child. However, these successful cases shared at least two of these factors:

(a) an experienced school administrator with several years on the job; (b) an administrator with a strong background in gifted education; (c) a rural school; (d) a small school; (e) a Montessori school; (f) a school without a reputation for being a "best practices" school; (g) a parent with good rapport in the school evidenced in mutual respect between school personnel and the family; and (h) a child with a more "extraordinary" level of intelligence (IQ>160). (Rogers, 2005, p. 16)

Take an active role in schoolwide activities to meet other committed parents, and simultaneously get to know other school personnel, all the while making a contribution to the education your child receives. Parent-teacher organizations, extracurricular clubs, and afterschool activities always can use more parental involvement. Parents who take part benefit by becoming more familiar with their child's classmates and teachers, and possibly also by learning how to interact effectively with particular school personnel.

Join Like-Minded Parents in an Advocacy Group

If there is an organization that supports the needs of gifted students, join it. Such organizations often vary in strength from one year to the next as particular parents move in and out of the group, but they offer your best source for learning what educational modifications have or have not been done for other children in the school your child attends.

By joining an advocacy group, you will strengthen its impact. As such groups gain members, their potential effectiveness increases not only by sheer numbers, but also because they are more likely to be able to work with school personnel over several years' time. Members become familiar with school personnel, learn how the local schools are organized, and discover the best channels through which to affect change (Davidson Institute for Talent Development, 2005).

The staff of the Davidson Institute for Talent Development offers suggestions to help parent advocacy groups work effectively with schools. (See http://www.geniusdenied.com for examples.) The steps in the table at the end of this chapter are adapted from their materials (see Table 13).

Share Your Strengths

Particular grades or even individual classes may also benefit from your attention. If you happen to have a particular area of expertise, teachers may be interested in having you talk with the class about it when they are studying a related topic. If you have your own business, you may be able to donate materials or labor the school needs. This not only strengthens the school and your relationship with it, but it may also give you a tax deduction.

Examine Your Attitude

Even if you cannot contribute much to the classroom directly, keep in mind that some approaches will be more or less successful than others when you interact with your child's teachers. First and foremost, recognize that most people who become teachers do so because they want to make a difference in children's lives. Teachers want to provide an appropriate environment to help children learn, and they have spent their professional lives learning how to do this well.

Treat teachers with the same respect you would accord other professionals, and be sure to recognize their commitment and expertise. Table 13 provides more tips for advocating effectively for your child's education.

Table 13
An 8-Step Guide to Effective Parent Advocacy

Action Step	Tips for Implementation
Identify parents whose children have similar educational needs and arrange a meeting.	Recruit parents of children in the science class; parents at a local science fair; parents in 4-H, Scouts, etc.
Determine your general goals and the specific educational services your children need.	Brainstorm—self-contained classrooms? Dual enrollment of middle school students in the high school science classes?
Identify options that are least expensive and easiest for the school to implement.	Think creatively—dual enrollment? grade acceleration? Subject acceleration? (Refer to Rogers (2005) for more examples)
Develop a strategy for how to approach the school or the district.	Read articles on educational advocacy; share them with your group.
Identify 3–5 representatives from the group to be the principal negotiators.	Get to know each other, and this will be relatively intuitive.
Practice your pitch and responses to potential objections.	Role play in the group; brainstorm about possible objections.
Arrange a meeting and discuss viable solutions with school administrators.	Try for win-win situations. Above all, stay calm and rational. Don't show negative emotions.
Follow up.	Stay actively involved to be sure that your plans are implemented.

Compiled from Davidson Institute for Talent Development, 2005.

Chapter 5

Modifying Education for Your Scientifically Advanced Child

How many times has the thought entered your mind that your child may have different needs in school compared with other students of the same age? Perhaps instead of trying to fit your child into their mold, you should work to modify that mold so that it better fits your own child.

Educational modifications are mandated for students in special education situations but rarely legislated for advanced students. Some schools may be reluctant to offer the additional instruction you feel your child needs. Some schools or teachers may be unwilling even to admit that highly able students have different instructional needs than average students.

At the low end of the ability spectrum, students in special education programs clearly both need and benefit from differentiated instruction. However, our society often is hesitant to admit that there also are relevant individual differences at the high end of the ability spectrum. Those who argue against providing accelerated education programs may suggest that each child should have the same educational opportunities in a democratic society. The alternative viewpoint is that each child should be provided with an appropriate education that meets his or her individual needs.

If you have established a respectful relationship before such a situation arises, school personnel will be more likely to seriously consider your requests for a more individualized education for your child (Rogers, 2005). Then you will be in a better position to put to use the information you will learn in the following sections.

Would Your Child Benefit From Differentiated Instruction?

Boredom is one classic symptom of an advanced student who is not being challenged in school, but first rule out other causes. Children also say they are bored for a variety of other reasons that may include being tired, frustrated, or simply uninterested (Deal, 2003). However, when coupled with a sudden drop in school performance—particularly from very high-level to approximately average work—reports of boredom may indicate a child who needs and can benefit from a greater degree of *differentiation* in school. That is, he or she needs a modification of the one-size-fits-all curriculum. As a general rule, the farther ahead of his or her peers your child is, the more differentiation he or she will need (Winner, 1997). (The term *differentiated instruction* is preferred over the term *individualized instruction*, because you or your school may be able to identify a number of other children who face the same situation as your child and might benefit from the same modifications.)

Differentiation usually has two components, *diagnosis* and *instruction*. Diagnosis involves determining how much differentiation is needed and in what areas it is needed. Instruction involves ways to deliver modifications to the student. Some formal approaches to diagnosis are covered in Chapter 1.

> Differentiation = modification of a generalized curriculum to address specialized needs.

After you have evidence suggesting that your child needs differentiated instruction, the next step is to work with the school and teachers to determine how it will be carried out. You have a number of options. One resource for acceleration options is Vol. 2 of *A Nation Deceived: How Schools Hold Back America's Brightest Students* (Colangelo et al., 2004). Common solutions may range from giving pretests prior to instruction or simply finding ways to accommodate your child's science interest and ability into other coursework, to structural modifications such as changing to a more challenging teacher or skipping a grade. Consider some of the possibilities presented in Table 14.

Compact the Curriculum

Curriculum compacting is such a logical and well-supported idea for all children that one has to wonder at the amount of resistance it often receives, perhaps because of perceived teacher workload. It simply involves using a pretest to determine which students already know the material in question. Children who

	Table 14 **Steps Involved in Setting up a Differentiated Curriculum for Your Child**
Step	Example
Diagnosis	• Standardized testing • Classroom grades and test scores • Above-level testing as offered through various talent search programs
Instruction	• Curriculum compacting • Changing class level or teacher • Skipping a grade • Incorporating science interests into other subject areas

demonstrate mastery on a pretest of subject matter are allowed to study more advanced topics while the rest of the class learns the regular curriculum (Reis & Renzulli, 2005; Reis et al., 1993). This approach is quite similar to the DT-PI approach described in Chapter 2 (Stanley, 1978, 1998), but curriculum compacting uses a broader array of evidence of mastery, works with a broader array of subjects, and formally documents the acceleration or enrichment activities each student will undertake.

> Curriculum compacting = allowing students to study more advanced topics instead of repeating instruction that evidence shows they already know.

Change Placement in Current Courses

In many cases, changing a child's class level (as from regular to advanced) or classroom (and thus teacher) within the same course level may provide enough differentiation for moderately advanced students. Although curriculum is increasingly mandated by the states, the instruction that takes place often varies greatly from one classroom to the next depending on the teacher's knowledge, experience, and even personality. In smaller schools, the choice of teachers or classrooms may be limited by the size of the school, but the possibility of this type of differentiation should be kept in mind.

Be prepared to use persuasion and negotiation. School personnel who would willingly switch another child's classroom placement on behavioral grounds often will refuse on general principle to switch a child's classroom placement within a class level for simple instructional needs. Accommodation is usually most easily made at the beginning of the school year, when a lot of swapping about is going on for other reasons such as late arrivals and adjustments in class size.

Changing placement is not a new idea, but it can work very well. For example, early into one school year, my alert mother talked our elementary school into switching classrooms for two of my siblings. One was taking undue advantage of a teacher's relaxed teaching style and needed the structure provided in a more disciplined classroom; the other would have been a nervous wreck in the structured classroom, but thrived under placement in the more relaxed environment.

Move Across Grades

Colangelo et al. (2004) suggest that grade skipping, or *acceleration,* is perhaps the best single option available for meeting the educational needs of highly able students. It is most commonly used at the elementary or middle school level, because high school students have other options such as dual enrollment, advanced placement classes, or early entry into college.

Acceleration is not the right solution for every student, of course, but for many it can be very appropriate. Three important questions should be addressed when considering accelerated placement:

1. Has the student's ability been assessed properly?
2. Given these assessment results, what is the most appropriate form of acceleration?
3. What can the school do to ensure this student's success if acceleration is used? (Colangelo et al., 2004).

If you have additional questions about whether your student in grades K–8 should be moved up a grade, consult the *Iowa Acceleration Scale* (Assouline, Colangelo, Lupkowski-Shoplik, Lipscomb, & Forstadt, 2003). You might also consider reading the Colangelo et al. report, *A Nation Deceived: How Schools Hold Back America's Brightest Students*, available as a free download at http://www.nationdeceived.org.

If you choose grade skipping for your highly able child who needs a more challenging classroom experience, be prepared for the possibility of opposition from schools or teachers. It is usually much easier to get schools to demote students from higher to lower grade levels than it is to move them up.

At the upper grade levels, opposition often is based on the fact that successful completion of regular-level classes does not meet the course prerequisites that have been established for advanced-level classes. In such cases, test scores or other subject-specific evidence of mastery may be useful in helping schools make an appropriate decision.

Although research strongly supports the effectiveness of grade skipping, schools and teachers are often reluctant to use this intervention because they fear it will have a negative impact on students' social development. These fears are unfounded in most cases. Careful research over many years has shown that children allowed to skip a grade generally do well both mentally and socially. I myself skipped sixth grade, and except for the minor inconvenience of having to wait a bit longer than my friends to get a driver's license, the overall experience was quite beneficial.

Learn Science in Other Subjects

An additional approach to curricular differentiation seldom addressed in the education literature is to integrate science learning into other content areas such as English (Thier & Daviss, 2002) or social studies. Even art or physical education classes present opportunities for the motivated science learner. With some encouragement, the student who is strongly interested in science,

> Encourage your student to relate learning in other areas to the disciplines that interest him or her.

whether in general or in a particular scientific field, will likely do everything in his or her power to make other classes relevant to these interests.

Not all interested students will be capable of seeing these other classes as potential opportunities, however, and some otherwise bright students may fail to achieve good grades in classes that do not interest them. This pattern of differential achievement may make it more difficult for students who wish to be admitted to a particular college to study a specific area that interests them. Parents and teachers both can and should encourage students to develop the ability to relate their learning in other areas to the disciplines that interest them, and should maintain ongoing communications with one another in case these changes still fail to improve the student's performance.

Work together, and think creatively. As an example, high school social studies lessons about European history may at first have little to hold the attention of the student who is obsessively interested in analytical chemistry. However, there are in fact many ways in which these two interests may overlap. A student might review the varied chemical investigations attempting to establish the validity of the Vinland Map, a map that clearly depicts the New World, yet apparently dates to many years before Columbus' explorations. In studying the 18th and 19th century, the same student might wish to learn how social and political changes affected the emergence of the chemical dye industry in different European countries. Each of these projects would require the student to understand the relevant social studies content, but would also lead to more in-depth knowledge related to the student's interests in analytical chemistry. If parents or teachers do not have the time or expertise to suggest such curricular modifications, they should try to find a mentor who is interested and capable to work on these projects with the student.

Many children have multiple interests, and these should be encouraged. However, being single-minded is OK, too. The late Dr. E. Paul Torrance, who spent most of his long and productive lifetime observing and working with gifted and creative children, offered a rationale for an appropriately differentiated education based on his experience. Torrance (1983) gave the following advice in his *Manifesto for Children*: "Know, understand, take pride in, practice, develop, exploit and enjoy your greatest strengths. . . . Don't waste energy trying to be well rounded. Do what you love and can do well" (p. 1).

Supplementing or Replacing
Traditional School Options

I myself am a graduate of the public school system and urge you to work within this system first if you can, but I readily concede that for some students other options are worth exploring. Sometimes these can be used alongside public school attendance; in other cases, they may be a substitute for it.

Investigate Charter and Magnet Schools

One educational trend that has been implemented widely over the past decade is the establishment of special schools. For the student with strong interests and abilities in a particular field, special schools can be an attractive educational option. Many special schools are available for students in grades K–12, with some extending into dual enrollment with college programs. Because they are publicly funded, there usually is little added expense compared to the regular public school setting.

Charter schools are allowed to operate within a school district but are governed independently of most of the bureaucracy that controls the operation of traditional public schools. Charter schools are designed to encourage innovative responses to the problems faced in traditional schools by allowing the founders of the school (those granted the charter) a great degree of control over the school's budget, curriculum, and staffing. The teachers in charter schools may or may not be required to obtain the same training that teachers have in traditional public schools. State laws regulate the processes for establishing charter schools and govern the relationship between charter schools and the school districts in which they are located.

Magnet schools offer classes in all subject areas but focus on developing students' talents in one or two areas. For example, one magnet school may emphasize ecology; another, the performing arts. These schools usually draw students from a wide geographic area. Students from an entire district or sometimes even an entire state may be able to attend the same magnet school. Administratively, magnet schools are often run by the regular school district. Because they tend to interest mainstream students, magnet schools often are developed in school buildings where districts are having difficulty attracting nonminority attendees. The diverse student body at these schools stands in contrast to many neighborhood schools, which tend to be more ethnically homogeneous.

Districts often provide some form of transportation for students who attend magnet schools. Magnet schools may be located quite a distance from where students live, particularly in larger districts. This can make it more difficult for parents to interact face-to-face with school personnel. If transportation is not provided, you will need to consider this added difficulty and expense in making the decision to have your child attend a special school. Another possible issue is that statewide magnet programs, particularly at the high school level, tend to be residential programs. These, too, call for parental attention to logistics and to any possible social and emotional issues that may be relevant to a given child's situation.

Charter and magnet schools have grown at a tremendous pace in recent years. Learn about these schools, their specialties, and their admissions procedures. Some magnet schools have a competitive admissions process that requires a complex application, possibly including essays, interviews, or a portfolio of student work. Other special schools may have a lottery-based admissions process if the demand for the school is high. Plan well in advance. Either of these types of admission process will likely require parental action 6 months or more before the start of the school year.

If there is a strong community demand but no appropriate school available, you may wish to consider organizing a group of parents to look into the possibility of advocating for the establishment of a special school in your area. The degree of involvement that will be required varies widely, ranging anywhere from short-term organized advocacy efforts aimed at convincing a district to establish a magnet school, to serving on the governing board of a charter school. The possibility of establishing a unique school offers an important yet complex and time-consuming option in the search for an appropriate education for your child.

Consider Distance Education

Distance education, sometimes also called distance learning, describes any educational program in which the student and teacher are in different locations when instruction is taking place. Originally, these programs were disseminated via the mail, radio, telephone, fax, or interactive satellite video. Today, however, with the recent explosive growth of the Internet, the majority of distance education programs are delivered online.

Distance education programs offer a particularly useful option when families are traveling and are unable to attend a regular school, yet wish to have a formal record of their child's learning. Parents who homeschool their children also find distance learning quite helpful as a means of providing their children access to advanced coursework that they may not feel capable of teaching themselves.

Increasingly, distance learning also is being used to deliver advanced coursework to students whose districts are too small or too isolated to offer these classes within the regular school schedule. It also allows students to take classes in subjects that interest them, but that are not generally offered in public school.

A distinction should be made between independent learning and distance learning: In independent learning, students are primarily responsible for working through a course of study or other organized content on their own initiative. Learning materials are available commercially, in a variety of formats from textbook to DVD, but purchase of the materials does not include any teaching, tutoring, or other assistance. Distance learning, in contrast, includes both the course material itself and one or more forms of personal or small-group assistance to help the student master its content.

Program Types

Distance learning usually operates in one of two ways. In *asynchronous* designs, students and instructors do not usually interact at the same time. For example, a student may pose a question in the afternoon, and then the teacher posts a reply that evening that the student reads the following morning. In contrast, *synchronous* distance learning requires both the student and teacher to interact during a shared meeting time. A conference call would be one form of synchronous interaction. In online terms, chat rooms are synchronous, while discussion boards are asynchronous. Internet technology makes synchronous designs much easier to implement than they used to be, and most online classes now are made up of a combination of synchronous and asynchronous components.

> Synchronous distance learning involves direct real-time interaction between teacher and student. Asynchronous programs have more flexibility.

The Four C's of Choosing a Program

Regardless of the reason for choosing to enroll in a distance education class, there are several points to consider when selecting a distance education program. *Cost* is a major factor for many parents, and should perhaps be the first consideration. Costs vary widely with the program, ranging from essentially no cost to as much as thousands of dollars per class. Costs depend on a variety of factors that may include the nature of the organization that is sponsoring the class, the instructor's qualifications, the number of instructional and credit hours involved, and whether textbooks and other materials and supplies are included. Some distance learning programs offer financial aid, although many do not.

Another question to ask yourself is how *compatible* is the program with your child? This issue includes both the nature of the coursework, and the match between the course delivery style (method and timing) with the schedule and learning needs of your child. The scientifically motivated child will need a class that offers appropriate science content taught at a pace and in a style she can easily follow. A course that is primarily asynchronous will be a more appropriate choice for the busy high school student than one that is mostly synchronous, because a synchronous schedule would be likely to conflict with the student's prior commitments to other activities. Younger students, whose schedules may be a bit less regimented, may benefit from the more structured learning environment that synchronous interaction allows.

Course credit and *accreditation* of the distance education program are important because they determine how the regular school will (or in some cases, will not) recognize the work your child has completed. The work your child does through an accredited, credit-granting institution can be included on his transcript in the same manner as any other credit transferred from another school. Programs that are accredited by a regional accreditation agency, such as the Southern Association of Colleges and Schools (SACS), can grant school credit and issue transcripts in the same manner as any regular brick and mortar school. If you are not familiar with the accreditation reported by a program, a list of recognized accreditation agencies in higher education can be found online (see http://www.chea.org/public_info).

Not all distance education programs are accredited or need to be, however. Programs whose offerings consist primarily of specialized enrichment classes, as opposed to the more typical classroom subjects, may not need to be accredited or need to grant credit. If they did, most schools would not know what to do with such hours other than perhaps use them as electives. For other programs, particularly small ones, seeking accreditation would impose a significant drain on resources that might better be used to improve the quality of their programs.

If your child wishes to be awarded credit for participating in a program that does not grant credit, it is often possible to petition your child's school or school district to grant it. Usually this process will require the program in question to supply a course syllabus and a description of how many hours of instruction were involved. Some type of evaluation of the child's performance is also necessary. Acceptable evidence may include a grade, a written evaluation of performance, or (in some subject areas) a standardized achievement test score obtained by your child after completing the program. Because the process of granting credit varies greatly from one school district to the next, if credit is an important part of your child's educational plan, your safest course of action is to check with the school ahead of time to be sure that the course your child is considering will be acceptable.

Finally, a word of *caution* is in order. Although the majority of distance-learning providers are reputable, a few are not. Disreputable programs have profited for many years by conferring bogus degrees on anyone willing to pay for them. There seems little likelihood at present that these organizations would target children seeking rigorous courses in science, because a common feature of bogus programs is that little to no actual work is required of students. Nevertheless, buyer beware. There are several good articles available on the Web that discuss how to determine whether or not a program is legitimate. For examples, see http://www.elearners.com/resources/diploma-mills.asp and http://geteducated.com/articles/degreemills.asp.

Look Into Dual Enrollment

In addition to the variety of summer and distance-learning options, many colleges and universities offer the option of dual enrollment. Dual enrollment is technically more acceleration than enrichment, but it ultimately serves both purposes. Stated briefly, dual enrollment allows a student who has completed the available high school curriculum in an area to enroll in one or more college classes part-time while remaining in high school for other classes as appropriate. Dual enrollment is most common in math and physics courses, but may also be appropriate for students with advanced ability, interests, and completed coursework in chemistry, biology, anatomy, and other science classes.

Dual enrollment is most commonly used for providing classes after students have successfully completed the school's Advanced Placement coursework in a particular subject. This option is also useful for students who wish to take classes that are not available at their high school. One real advantage to dual enrollment is that these courses carry college credit, in most cases readily transferable to the student's permanent record at any university.

No college nearby? Ask questions. In many cases, instructional options such as distance learning for college-level courses are also available as dual enrollment options.

Search Out Summer Programs

For the scientifically motivated child who is fortunate enough to attend a school that effectively meets his or her educational needs, summer programs can be like the frosting on the cake. For other children, a summer program may be the cake itself. Either way, summer programs fill an important role in further educating the scientifically advanced child.

Summer programs come in many varieties. Some specifically target gifted and/or scientifically advanced students. Many other programs seek to develop talent and career interests among student groups that traditionally have been underrepresented in science, math, or technology. Still other programs are designed to enhance science education for all students at all levels.

Summer programs may be day-long or residential in approach. Residential programs generally cost quite a bit more than a comparable day program, but in return they usually provide meals and accommodations, as well as 24-hour supervision.

Investigate your options. Several online sources including the National Association for Gifted Children (http://www. nagc.org) offer lists of summer programs for able students. The *Educational Opportunity Guide* updated annually by the Duke University Talent Identification Program, offers a state-by-state directory of educational programs that includes many summer opportunities for academically able students. This publication can be ordered online at https://tipstore.tip.duke.edu/eog.asp.

If you happen to have a university nearby, check its Web site to learn about summer opportunities on campus. The Howard Hughes Medical Institute sponsors a variety of science learning initiatives through various universities. Some university science departments also offer similar programs.

Some states offer a particular type of summer program at little or no cost to participants. Often called a Governor's School, these tend to be offered to high school students through a competitive application process. The state of Georgia, for example, has offered the Governor's Honors Program for many years. Students who qualify as rising juniors or seniors spend 6 weeks studying their field of interest in depth, staying on a college campus at state expense. Your child's science teacher or school guidance counselor should know whether this type of program exists in your area.

Think About Homeschooling

Homeschooling is just what it sounds like: Children receiving schooling in their home, usually taught primarily by a parent. In a sense, this is what you've been giving your child since birth. As an involved parent, every time you follow the suggestions in this book or help your child understand their schoolwork, you're doing supplemental homeschooling, as well. The step from here to total responsibility for your child's education is a big one, but it's also a continuation of a direction in which you're already traveling.

Full-time homeschooling, in which all instruction occurs at home rather than through classes at a public or private school, has grown tremendously over the past two decades. Nationwide, 1.1 million students (about 2.2% of all school-aged children) were being homeschooled in 2003 (Princiotta, Bielick, & Chapman, 2004).

Traditionally, parents have opted for homeschooling due to either religious or philosophical differences with public schooling. Although these reasons still apply in many cases, much of the recent growth in homeschooling has come as a way for parents to ensure that the individual learning needs of their child are met (Kearney, 2004).

Public school teachers often disparage homeschooling. However, statistics suggest that homeschooled students' achievement test scores in general tend to be well above average (Rudner, 1999). Recent well-publicized examples of homeschooled students who have won national spelling bees, been admitted to prestigious universities, or become university valedictorians suggest that many children are served quite well by being educated at home.

Homeschooling allows students to learn new material at their own pace, without pressure from classmates who may learn more slowly or more quickly. Homeschooling also allows considerable flexibility in pursuing students' individual interests in science or other fields of study. Considering curricular pacing, it only makes sense that a ratio of one parent for each one, two, or even half a dozen children would provide a more individualized learning environment than one teacher can offer for 20 to 30 or more children within the regular classroom.

As has been the case with acceleration (grade skipping), much of the traditional opposition to homeschooling has been directed toward its perceived potential for harming children's social development. As the movement has grown, however, this concern has become much less relevant. Homeschooling in many areas now consists of networks rather than isolated families, and much instruction is now carried out within local groups of children in the same age group who share similar interests. Occasionally, some public schools also will allow homeschooled students to participate in extracurricular activities. Whether based on cooperative, religious, or other principles, these arrangements allow children to experience a full range of social interaction with their peers.

Homeschooling should not be undertaken without a lot of serious thought. Only you and your child can know whether it would be right for both of you. For the child whose needs are not being met in school, and whose parents can make the necessary commitments of time, energy, and money, homeschooling may be one of the most effective options available. It can make a tremendous difference in your child's life, even if you only use this option for a year or two.

Good background articles are available that discuss the process (see Ensign, 1997). State Department of Education Web sites generally describe the regulations that apply, and may also list local contacts in the homeschooling community. For a complete picture of what would be involved, find and talk with other homeschooling parents in your community.

— Chapter **6** —

Helping Your Child With Science Fairs and Other Research-Based Competitions

I ndependent research projects can play an extremely important role in the scientifically talented student's development. In addition to developing particular skills, such research projects can allow students to become recognized as experts in a particular subject area. It is also worth mentioning that college admissions officials generally recognize the substantial extracurricular effort that independent research requires, and tend to look favorably on students who have successfully completed science fair projects or other similar competitions. The American

Association for the Advancement of Science (AAAS) recommends that:

> Before graduating from high school, students working individually or in teams should design and carry out at least one major investigation. They should frame the question, design the approach, estimate the time and costs involved, calibrate the instruments, conduct trial runs, write a report, and, finally, respond to criticism. (1993, Section B, ¶ 4–5)

These experts suggest that such investigations might take weeks or even months to complete, and may require work both in and out of school. Although the above recommendation is directed primarily at high school students, authorities suggest that independent research projects can be undertaken successfully by academically talented children as young as 9 or 10 years old (Kellett, 2005).

Independent research experience and competitions are valuable pursuits for scientifically advanced children. Being constrained to follow a recognized format, meet a deadline, compare one's efforts with others, and explain one's work in public are all important learning experiences that will help any student with later success in his or her life and career.

Your child will find that the approaches and tactics outlined here can be applied to a wide variety of future school projects and even to future careers in many different fields. You may be surprised to hear that writing may actually be the most important skill a child develops by doing such projects. It is the one activity that ties all the others together, and it is the most transferable of the varied skills students practice in the course of completing a project. The particular observational or measurement techniques and even the field of study itself may change as the student grows older and develops new interests, but writing skills will always remain necessary and useful. By writing scientific works, and by reading scientific writing by others, students move toward an internalized understanding of the conventions of scientific study. Through reading and writing over many projects and many years of study, students come to recognize and learn to apply the shared conventions that make scientific communication possible.

Because of the sustained individual effort that projects of this type require, effective guidance is vital if students are to achieve successful outcomes. Where will this come from? You guessed it! Although teachers and other mentors often can provide assistance, even in this best-case scenario your timely assistance and encouragement will undoubtedly be required. With younger students who may not yet have any teachers who specialize in science, your parental guidance will be absolutely necessary if your child is to get the most out of the experience.

In the pages that follow, you'll be introduced to the general processes and time frame to expect. This chapter focuses on the science fair project because this special type of project is ideal for meeting the learning needs of the scientifically able student. However, these suggestions will also help you help your child be successful with other similar research-based independent learning activities.

Understanding Science Fairs and Similar Competitions

A science fair project represents a relatively common, yet specialized genre of independent study. Students in upper elementary grades usually work in teams, while older students more commonly complete individual projects.

Science fairs are competitions typically conducted at different levels, from the local classroom, school, or district level all the way to national and international competitions. Winners of fairs at the lower levels typically are invited to compete at the higher and more competitive levels. If your child's school does not sponsor a fair and your child is still interested in participating, it is usually possible to enter at the next level of competition. Check with fair officials.

Science fair projects can be distinguished from other types of independent projects by three primary characteristics: (1) the research focus of the projects themselves, which requires that students generate new knowledge related to their topic; (2) the specific format in which this work is presented, which is to say, as an exhibit that includes a display board, laboratory notebook, and formal research report; and (3) the science fair itself, which is a day-long event in which projects conducted by different students are evaluated by panels of judges.

Choosing a Project Wisely

The keys to a successful research project sound deceptively simple: choose a feasible, appropriate, and safe topic; collect data in a scientifically defensible manner; document the project effectively; and be able to explain the project to interested people. However, if you and your child have never been involved in undertaking such a project, it can seem quite daunting. Here are some tips to make it all easier.

Allow Enough Time

The first, and perhaps most important, key to any successful project is to allow sufficient time to complete it. Two to three months is a realistic time frame for conducting a science fair project. At the more competitive state and national levels, most students will have developed their work over the course of an entire year.

Experienced teachers recognize that an extended time frame produces better results and is less stressful for students. These teachers generally will offer grades or other feedback on an ongoing basis, and will break down the process into a series of manageable steps for their students.

If you are reading this advice too late to apply it, go ahead and provide the emotional encouragement and practical support your child needs to make a run for the finish line anyway, rather than giving up. Teaching your child that he can still come through in a pinch also is a valuable life lesson. (Above all, though, don't be tempted to do the project for your child. That's a horrible lesson and precedent.)

It is actually possible to develop and carry out an adequate project over as little as one extended weekend. I can almost guarantee you, however, that doing so will burn out you and your child to the degree that you both vow never to do a project that way again.

Will the Project Be Feasible, Appropriate, and Safe?

What will your child work with? For most children, this is the first decision, and for many, an enthusiastic and passionate one: "I want to study my goldfish! I want to build a bridge! I want to make dynamite!"

The best science fair projects generally are those done by students who have a strong and genuine interest in the topic they are investigating. But, beyond interest, the topic also must be feasible. No matter how interested your child may be in the geology of Mars, you probably won't be able to help him or her go there to conduct an experiment. Rather than just adopting your child's first idea, spend some time talking about issues of safety, suitability, and the hassle factor. Some entities are definitely easier to work with than others.

Project ideas that involve areas such as chemistry, electricity, radiation, or molds and microorganisms require special efforts because of safety concerns. Many chemicals, devices such as lasers, and other potentially dangerous materials will also require special approval before the project can be started. Information about and the necessary forms to gain approval are available online in many states. Many local fairs will adhere to the ISEF rules, which can be downloaded from http://www.sciserv.org/isef/document.

You may want to consider sidestepping the potential problems involved by encouraging your child to consider changing the nature of the project at the outset. However, if you do get the OK for a project in one of these areas of safety concern, realize that before your child begins an experiment, you will need to review her procedures carefully. Have the teacher review them, as well. The safety concerns presented in Table 15 are only a sample. Be sure your child understands and follows all the safety procedures needed for his or her own project.

Many students want to use household pets or other people in their project. However, this can be a hassle. Special rules must be followed in experiments using humans. Nothing may be done that is likely to cause them harm. Participation should be voluntary. Special signed forms, approvals, and procedures are involved; again, they usually must be submitted before the work starts. (Some experiments, like those that just involve observing people, may be exempt, but may need to be submitted for approval anyway to make this determination.)

Experiments with fish, amphibians, reptiles, birds, and mammals (i.e., any vertebrate animal) also follow special

> Consider projects that require few or no preapproval forms and special permissions.

Table 15
Science Project Safety Concerns

Subject Studied	Safety Concern and Advice
Chemicals	Answers to safety questions can be found in laboratory manuals or chemical catalogs such as the *Flinn Chemical Catalog and Reference Manual*. Most schools also have information sheets on the chemicals used in science classes. These are called Material Safety Data Sheets, or MSDS. MSDS also are often available online.
Molds and microorganisms	Proceed with a lot of caution and substantial guidance from a knowledgeable mentor. Uninvited microbial contaminants are always a possibility; most are harmless, but some are not.
Electricity	Avoid using current from household outlets; use batteries instead. Use as little voltage as possible. Make sure electrical appliances and tools are insulated and grounded.
Radiation	Remember, experiments using microwave ovens, lasers, radon, and some types of smoke detectors all involve radiation. Even in small amounts these could be harmful to living tissue. Get guidance from a knowledgeable individual. Know the law; certain state and federal laws may apply.

rules. Generally, a qualified adult trained in animal care must agree to oversee the project even before the first organism is obtained. Increasingly, a veterinarian's supervision is required.

Get a copy of the rules; read them before you even begin, and decide whether it is worth the potential aggravation. Studies involving humans or other vertebrate animals will require extra layers of approval before you can begin your project; if these approvals are not obtained ahead of time, the project will be disqualified from competing in most science fairs. Your child's science teacher or the school's science fair organizer will have the paperwork you need to fill out to get these approvals started, but be sure to allow extra time for the process.

Also consider what you will do with the experimental entities after the project is over. Robots could sit on a shelf in the garage forever, but are you prepared to clean gerbil cages for the rest of their natural life? Plants are great; no one will object if your child's bean plants are fed to a rabbit after testing how well different types of organic compost make them grow. Native invertebrates, from crickets and worms, to the little parasitoid wasps called WOWBugs (Matthews, Koballa, Flage, & Pyle, 1996), can safely be let go into your back yard after studying their behavior. Native plants, insects, and other arthropods are relatively easy to find, and can be used in any number of innovative science projects. Crickets and worms can be purchased in bulk at bait shops. Even cockroaches have been used successfully as research subjects in award-winning projects. Table 16 shows some of the advantages of using hassle-fee experimental subjects in your child's project. In most cases, a bit of creative thought about alternatives can make your experiments safer and simpler, and reduce the amount of paperwork you and your child will have to fill out to do them.

Define the Project: "Effect" Is the Magic Word

Once your child has identified an interesting invertebrate, plant, object, or other subject to experiment with, he has to figure out what to do with it. If your child has never done an independent

Table 16
The Three Most Hassle-Free Experimental Subjects for Science Fair Projects

Potential Subject	Examples	Advantages
Invertebrates (animals without backbones)	Fruitflies, WOWbugs, crickets, caterpillars, pillbugs (roly-poly bugs), and worms	Small, easily housed, require no special permits, easily released when project is finished
Plants	Beans, bedding plants, houseplants, Fast Plants (http://www.fastplants.org for more information)	Easily obtained or grown from seed, do not escape, easy to replicate, can be maintained or composted when project is finished
Nonliving objects	Household items, models, robots	Easily obtained or made, do not escape or die (but may break down), generally no permits or special safety concerns, disposal not generally an issue

research project, he may have trouble going beyond this point to pinpoint a specific research problem. If so, skip ahead to the Four Question Strategy in the section, "What to Do When You Have No Idea What to Do." However, if your child already has identified a general research idea, picking a title can be a great way to start defining the project more fully.

Word the proposal as a question, using the form "What is/ are the effect(s) of _____ on _____?" Be as specific as possible.

Include the things you will measure (see below). For example, rather than just "What are the effects of fertilizer on plants?" ask "What is the effect of fertilizer dosage on soybean plant root growth?" Now it's clear that you'll be measuring dosages and root growth.

Titles sometimes also benefit from adding another short statement at the end of the main question, to clarify the purpose or conditions of the experiment. For example, the above message might be clarified by adding "during different growing seasons."

Coming up with the title at the beginning of the project accomplishes two things at once. It defines the project, and it also gives a title under which to present the results.

This title-first approach also helps determine the steps that must come next; based on the sample title in the previous paragraph, it should be clear that this project will require fertilizer, soybean plants, and the time to conduct the tests during different growing seasons.

Plan to Repeat the Measurements

A whole host of errors can creep in if measurements are taken only once—experimenter blunders such as writing down the wrong number, systematic slip-ups such as failing to consider that plants may have different growth rates even under the same environmental conditions, or a variety of other types of errors (see Allchin, 2001). Repeating measurements may be the single most effective way to reduce the influence of many of these sources of potential error.

> Repetition is an important part of good experimental design. How many trials are enough? There is no magic number. In general, more is better.

With some types of projects, measurements can be repeated using the same experimental entity. For example, the robot can be run up the same slope a dozen times. In other cases, the entities themselves must be repeated. To determine bean plant growth 3 days after fertilization, one needs to obtain the average value for a dozen bean plants; it's not enough to just measure a single plant over and over a dozen times on day three.

The "dozen" number was pulled out of a hat. Unfortunately, there is no single magic number of times to repeat an experiment or measurement to ensure sufficient results. It will depend on the type of experiment, the nature of the data, and the field of study. In chemistry laboratory practice, for example, three repetitions would be considered a good minimum number for a relatively simple but labor-intensive procedure such as an acid-base titration. However, if the first three measurements did not agree with one another sufficiently well, a fourth measurement would be appropriate. Because the main source of differences in the values would probably be human error in conducting the procedure, a chemist might assume that if three of these four measures were in close agreement but the fourth was quite different, the three that were similar were better approximations of the quantity that is being measured.

In contrast, a project measuring plant growth might need 10 or more plants in each experimental condition. More than the measurement process is involved in the differences observed in their varying growth rates. Rarely would the biological researcher discard any measurement. However, if it seemed justified for reasons that had little to do with the research (e.g., one plant got knocked over and never quite recovered), the omission in the data would be clarified with a footnote.

In general, more is better. (In research with human health, scientists often have thousands of repetitions!) Regardless of the experiment, fewer than three repetitions will not be considered adequate by many science fair judges.

Judges often will question students about potential sources of error in project results, and the student who can demonstrate an understanding of the need for multiple trials will probably receive higher marks. In some fairs, the use of repetitions is also formalized on the grading scale that the judges use. Your child can ask her science teacher or mentor to help her figure out how many repetitions might be appropriate for her particular project, but if their advice seems off the mark, be prepared to offer your own input, as well.

Control Other Variables

Good study designs should eliminate or minimize the possible effects of variables other than those the child intends to investigate. Below are a few of the most common ways scientists control their experimental conditions.

Replication

As mentioned above, simply using many entities in each treatment group will help cancel out random variation, such as different rates of growth from one plant to the next.

Control Groups

Including parallel entities that don't receive any treatment at all (controls) will show what would happen normally in the absence of the treatment. For example, plants may grow in average soil or even in water alone, so it should be obvious that not all of the growth of the group that was fertilized was due to the fertilizer treatment alone. By setting up the experiment to include one group of plants that are fertilized and one group that are not, one can better tell how much of the growth is normal versus how much may be explained by the experimental treatment.

Standardized Conditions

Providing standardized conditions can be a particular challenge when working with humans or with intelligent animals. Scientists the world over know the cautionary tale of Clever Hans, a horse that seemed to be able to do arithmetic (see the sidebar for the story of Clever Hans).

Making everything else the same is the only way to have any idea whether observed results are the consequence of the things that were changed on purpose. Experiments with living things, in particular, must be set up to minimize the effects (if any) of environmental differences. In our experiments involving plant growth and fertilizer, for example, every group would have to be kept under identical lighting, temperature, and rainfall.

Controlling for other variables can occasionally require substantial effort, as illustrated in the following example from Nobel-winning physicist Richard Feynman's well-known essay, "Cargo Cult Science":

> For example, there have been many experiments running rats through all kinds of mazes, and so on—with little clear result. But in 1937 a man named Young did a very interesting one. He

The Tale of Clever Hans

In the 1890s in Germany, a horse called Clever Hans baffled scientists and public audiences with his intellectual abilities, which included mathematics, an aptitude for identifying musical intervals, and a working knowledge of the German language. If someone were to ask him the square root of 16, Hans would dutifully reply with four taps of his hoof.

An investigating panel of two zoologists, a psychologist, a horse trainer, and a circus manager could find no flaw in the horse's talents. Indeed, Clever Hans seemed to be on the verge of embarrassing the entire scientific community until one young psychologist asked how Hans would perform if asked questions by someone who didn't know the correct answers. It was then that the horse's score plummeted to almost zero.

Clever Hans had not mastered mathematics, music, or German after all, but had in effect learned to read peoples' minds by observing subtle changes in their posture, breathing and facial expressions (Adapted from Carroll, 2005).

had a long corridor with doors all along one side where the rats came in, and doors along the other side where the food was. He wanted to see if he could train the rats to go in at the third door down from wherever he started them off. No. The rats went immediately to the door where the food had been the time before.

The question was, how did the rats know, because the corridor was so beautifully built and so uniform, that this was the same door as before? Obviously there was something about the door that was different from the other doors. So he painted the doors very carefully, arranging the textures on the faces of the doors exactly the same. Still the rats could tell. Then he thought maybe the rats were smelling the food, so he used chemicals to change the smell after each run. Still the rats could tell. Then he realized the rats might be able to tell by seeing the lights and the arrangement in the laboratory like any commonsense person. So he covered the corridor, and still the rats could tell.

He finally found that they could tell by the way the floor sounded when they ran over it. And he could only fix that by putting his corridor in sand. So he covered one after another of all possible clues and finally was able to fool the rats so that they had to learn to go in the third door. If he relaxed any of his conditions, the rats could tell.

Now, from a scientific standpoint, that is an A-number-one experiment. That is the experiment that makes rat-running experiments sensible, because it uncovers the clues that the rat is really using—not what you think it's using. And that is the experiment that tells exactly what conditions you have to use in order to be careful and control everything in an experiment with rat-running. (Feynman, 1974, ¶ 31–33).

Run a Reality Check

By starting with a potential project title and the work it implies, you and your child should easily be able to run a reality check on the proposed project right at the start. Don't skip this step—it's important.

Is the Project the Right Size?

At this point it should become apparent that some titles are just too limited or too ambitious, in which case it should still be relatively easy to modify them. Your title question "What is the effect of fertilizer dosage on soybean plant root growth?" might be amended to say "What is the effect of fertilizer dosage on soybean plant growth during the fall outdoor growing season in Zone 7?" This modified title conveys more precisely the actual intent of the project, and, as an added bonus, the title no longer implies a project that includes measuring growth rates during other times of year or in other climate zones.

Do We Have What We Need to Do This Work?

Unusual tools may be needed for some projects. Consider this issue now. Often mentors, parents, or teachers may be able to arrange for students to borrow specialized equipment. Other times, creativity becomes an important skill as students work to construct their own apparatus to fulfill the same purpose as expensive commercial equipment.

Is it Really Research or Just a Demonstration?

Many of the ideas that are recycled each and every year at school science fairs across the country—picture the classic model of a volcano—are really nothing more than demonstrations. A demonstration conveys clearly how something works, but does nothing else. For some types of competitions, a demonstration is the right approach, but for a science fair it is not appropriate. Science projects must include research.

At a minimum, for a project to be considered research, it must involve measuring how changing one thing affects the measured value of something else. To make the poor overused volcano a research project, one might investigate how changing the diameter of the central tube of the volcano affects the height of the eruption, keeping the amount of eruption-producing chemicals the same. One might also study how different dilutions of the chemicals cause the eruption to change in height, or in volume of bubbles that erupt. Incorporating any of these uses of measurement, studied across controlled changes of a single variable using repeated measurements, would make the project a very nice piece of research rather than simply a demonstration.

One of the best ways to tell if a project is research is to consider whether or not it results in new knowledge. Projects that have produced new information are quite likely to be research, while projects that have not are probably demonstrations.

Is There a Twist?

An award-winning research project nearly always incorporates some sort of twist, that is, something that makes your project unique or different from the projects other students might develop if they started with the same materials. Although extensive lists of projects are available in books and online, I have avoided including any of these sources here because they share a common shortcoming—most of the projects they list are not research and/or are not unique. Few things are less exciting to a science fair judge than encountering a whole row of nearly identical projects. What's more is that having a wide variety of projects gives all students a greater opportunity to learn from each other's work.

What to Do When You Have No Idea What to Do

When assigned the task of identifying a specific research problem, some students are gripped by panic. Others propose broad topics such as plants, insects, or chemistry. What does the term *specific research problem* mean to a scientist? How can you help your son or daughter change a general topic (or the total lack of a topic at all) into a quality original research problem?

No Cookbook Projects, Please!

Sometimes, students are given a book of science fair ideas as a supposed way out of this problem. They follow the project directions like a recipe. When the judge asks why a particular method was used, they can only answer, "That's what the book said to do."

This is not what your student needs. Instead, he needs a strategy to help develop an interesting topic into a well-designed experiment.

Try the Four Question Strategy

The strength of the Four Question Strategy approach (Cothron, Giese, & Rezba, 2000) is that it automatically results in a whole host of feasible project ideas on almost any given topic your child can come up with.

The easiest way to understand this strategy is to model it. Suppose your child has come up with the general topic of crickets. Begin by reading the following four questions and sample answers. Encourage rapid brainstorming but don't judge the quality of the ideas just yet. The more responses your child can list, the better experiment he or she will be able to design at the end.

Question 1: What materials are readily available for conducting experiments on <u>crickets</u>?

Crickets from the bait shop, clear shoeboxes for cages, dog food for them to eat, a clock, a ruler . . .

Question 2: What do <u>crickets</u> do?

They hop, they crawl, they fight, they sing, they sleep, they eat . . .

Question 3: How can I change the materials in Question 1 to affect the actions listed in Question 2?

Change the number of crickets in a cage, change the size of the cages, feed them different kinds of food . . .

Question 4: Based on what <u>crickets</u> do, how can I measure or describe the response of <u>crickets</u> to the change?

Count how many times they chirp in a certain length of time, measure them and see how fast they grow, weigh them, measure how fast they move or how many times they jump . . .

To design an experiment for a science project, your child only has to select one choice, such as "change the number of crickets" from the responses to Question 3. This will be the *independent variable*. Then select a *dependent variable* from Question 4, such as "count how many times they chirp." To make the experiment fair, all other responses to Question 3 must be kept the same. They become *constants* in the experiment.

The most effective experiments use only one independent variable and one dependent variable. Although it is possible to design more complex experiments with multiple independent and dependent variables, interpreting the outcome(s) becomes trickier.

Note that if you decide to use the Four Question Strategy, here's where the books of science fair project ideas can actually be of use. Because they provide a list of necessary materials and a description of the action that will occur, the books already answer Questions 1 and 2. Using something from these books, answer Questions 3 and 4 to generate an original experiment.

How to Generate Hypotheses

To write the hypothesis for an experiment, use this format:

If <u>independent variable chosen from Question 3</u> *increases/ decreases, then* <u>dependent variable selection from Question 4</u> *will increase/decrease/remain the same.*

In the case of our crickets experiment, one wording could be "If the number of crickets in a cage increases, then the number of times they chirp per minute will increase." Alternatively, "If the number of crickets in a cage increases, then the number of times they chirp per minute will decrease."

A second set of crickets, kept in a cage where everything is the same except that the numbers of crickets don't vary, serves as a *control group*. The actions of these crickets must be observed, too. Comparing the actions of the control group and the experimental group will help your child understand and explain the changes observed. For example, perhaps both sets of crickets suddenly quieted down in response to changes in lighting; without the control group, your child would have no way to know the quietness was not due to the change in number that he or she made.

Collecting Data

The questions that drive scientific inquiry are based on observations. In science, observation is the use of the senses—such as vision or hearing—to gather and record information about structures or processes.

Recorded observations are called *data*. (It's a plural word; the singular is *datum*.) Put another way, data are items of information. Observations are often recorded as measurements, also called *quantitative* data. Scientists worldwide use an international system of measurements based on the metric system. If your student's project is quantitative, it too will need to use measurements from this system rather than the more familiar inches, pounds, or gallons.

> Data are the bits and pieces of information that are used to address a question.

Data also may be qualitative—that is, in the form of descriptions instead of measurements. These data are usually documented with careful notes, often accompanied by photographs or video footage. Qualitative data must be very clearly organized, consistently recorded, and reliable if they are to be of use.

Data collection methods will vary widely depending on the project in question. Data might include anything from photos or transcriptions of video footage to graphic output from analytical instruments. Students will want to work with their teacher or mentor to decide what information they will need to collect to answer their title question, and to determine what equipment they will need to access to make their measurements.

Documenting the Project

Science fairs require students to follow a formalized and quite specific set of conventions for presenting their work. These conventions are based on how researchers in corporate and academic research settings convey their findings to one another and to the world at large. The three major components of this effort are the laboratory notebook, the formal report, and the poster presentation or "big board." Each of these components of the exhibit highlights a particular facet of the overall presentation.

The Lab Notebook

The lab notebook needs to be started on the first day of the project. Lab notebooks are characterized by a permanent (sewn) binding, and by pages that are numbered consecutively from the first to the last page in the book. Lab notebooks may be purchased with pre-printed page numbers, or students can number the pages themselves when they begin using the book.

Guidelines for presentation are almost always included in science fair application materials.

Lab notebooks provide the raw record of what students actually have done. They should be completed only in ink, handwritten. Each entry should be dated, and mistakes should be crossed through with a single line, but never scratched out or erased. No pages should ever be removed from a lab notebook.

In real research settings, lab books are important enough that they may be notarized at the end of each day's work. The lab notebook provides formal evidence of when and by whom a new idea or process was developed. In professional research settings, the contents of the lab notebook can determine who receives patent rights, and potentially the millions of dollars in royalties that may accompany them.

The Research Report

The research report is a typed document that presents an overview of the project and the results that were obtained. It is the most formal part of the project exhibit, and this formality can present a source of difficulty for students who are unfamiliar with academic writing conventions.

Science fair entry materials usually offer general guidance on format and may even specify such matters as the way to enter references, whether footnotes are permitted, and the proper ways to present figures and tables. Projects in the social sciences usually follow American Psychological Association style (APA; 2001). Physical and biological science projects often follow conventions outlined in a document called Uniform Requirements for Manuscripts Submitted to Biomedical Journals, which can be accessed at http://www.icmje.org.

Look through the written materials about the science fair early and often during the course of the project. If they provide little or no guidance on research report format, encourage your child to check with science fair organizers or with his teacher to learn which style is most appropriate for his project.

Commonly, the report will have six sections: an introduction, methods, results, discussion, conclusions, and list of references. Sometimes the results, discussion, and conclusions will be combined into a single section. Table 17 explains what each section of the research report should contain.

Learning to write to a particular format and follow a particular style provides great practice for a career in the sciences, particularly for those entering fields in which different journals require the use of different styles in manuscripts submitted for publication.

The Presentation

Science fair projects are presented in a poster-based exhibit format designed to help viewers quickly locate the studies that interest them within a vast sea of work. In many ways, this phase of the project is a valuable introduction and practice for public presen-

---

Table 17
Components of Science Project Reports

The project report almost always has six sections:
1. Introduction—the background to the project and why it is relevant or important;
2. Methods—how the research question was investigated;
3. Results—what happened when the methods were used;
4. Discussion—what the results seem to mean, including any limitations that the author is aware of;
5. Conclusion—a brief restatement of the findings and their importance, and suggestions as to directions that future research on this topic might take; and
6. References—a list of books, articles, Web sites, etc. that have been cited in the text.

---

tations your child may later be called upon to make in almost any field from business and industry, to government or academia.

Buy or Make an Exhibit Board

The exhibit board itself usually has three sides so that it will stand on its own on a table for viewing. Lightweight 3-sided display boards may be purchased inexpensively at office supply stores. They also can be constructed at home from heavy corrugated cardboard and duct tape, made with foam core board, or even built to be reusable using hinged sections of plywood covered with fabric. If you help your child make a board, you may want to construct a somewhat larger one than the standard office-supply model, so that there will be a little more room for text and pictures. Consult the rules for your particular science fair to learn what size limitations apply in your locale.

Present Material Cleanly and Clearly

The text on the board will be a shorter but essentially similar version of the text presented in the research report, but the board should be made more visually interesting by including such things as photos and colored graphs whenever possible. The research report may have been a bit long-winded. If so, encourage your child to edit the version put on the board. Point out that people viewing the board will not have the time to read much text. If they want more detail, they can pick up the research report, which will always be placed on the table by the exhibit.

Encourage your child to present his or her work in ways that will make it stand out—within the limits of good taste, of course. That well-chosen title will help. Make it large enough to read from some distance away. (Have your child actually try sample letter sizes on a piece of scrap paper before putting anything on the board itself.)

Encourage a clean presentation that is not cluttered with extraneous detail. Computers can be amazing tools for producing large fonts for titles, checking spelling and grammar, and resizing graphs and photos to fit the available board space. However, it is easy to get carried away with excessively ornate typefaces, cute text effects, or other design tools that may detract from the information the presentation is trying to convey.

Counsel your child to pay particular attention to graphs. Carefully recorded observations are important even on their own. However, some of the biggest breakthroughs in science have come when scientists have been able to put together many specific observations to reach a general conclusion, or generalization. To look for such generalizations, it often helps to put the data in a graph.

Good graphs should be bold enough to read from a few feet away. They must also use patterns or colors that stand out

> Almost all effective research projects involve some sort of graph.

from one another. Both directions (the x- and y-axes) need to be labeled clearly. There must be a title, and a key that explains what each line or color represents.

Photos should show their topic in clear focus and without extra background clutter. They each need a clear caption that explains what they show. Either black and white or color photos are acceptable. Take photos that show the processes and results, rather than those that emphasize your child doing the project. The rules and guidelines for some competitions may specify that the student's face not be identifiable in the photos; others don't care.

Neatness counts, if not as a specific scoring item, then clearly in the first impression it gives. However, this can be difficult for many children. Here's a tip for a simple technique your child can use for all sorts of school projects over the years. Don't write directly on the board at all. Instead, compose each block of text, picture, or other item of the display as a separate unit on a piece of paper. In this way, any errors or serious smudges are easy to correct without affecting other parts of the display.

Mount each of these units on a slightly larger background of colored construction paper or card stock. These then can be moved around freely on the display board. When the arrangement looks pleasing, use a glue stick, double-sided tape, or Velcro™ to affix them in place.

Increasingly, scientists are using computer-based presentation programs such as Microsoft PowerPoint® to prepare posters for scientific conferences. Such programs let them compose the entire posterboard as a single slide, which can be enlarged and printed on oversized paper by specialty photocopy shops.

Organize the Presentation on the Board

Pay attention to the order in which materials are presented on the board. They should appear in the same order as in the report—

left to right, the same way people read. Place the introduction and methods sections from top to bottom on the left section of the board. Results will take up most of the center section (which is often wider than the sections on either side). Place the discussion and conclusions top to bottom on the right-hand section.

> The presentation should clearly convey the purpose of the project at first glance. Organization helps.

What About Other Display Materials?

Can your child's cage full of praying mantises sit on the table by the board? What about the 8-foot-tall robot that he built? The 30 bean plants your daughter watered with various manure-based fertilizers? There are obviously a great many practical, aesthetic, and safety issues to be considered, and there may be institutional limits, as well. Check in advance with teachers and science fair organizers regarding the rules governing displays. When such additional materials are admissible, they can add a great deal of interest to the project display.

Electrical service to the project display tables is usually quite limited. Check in advance. However, if adequate electricity is available, displays can have additional dimensions even when the project itself did not involve power use. Often these include accent lighting to highlight a particular part of the exhibit. Animations, video footage, slides, and the like may be used to display items that fair rules do not allow to be present otherwise. Contestants may be required to furnish a grounded power strip with a fuse or breaker, and to demonstrate that all electrical equipment in the display has been UL listed. Fair rules specify, "Project sounds, lights, odors, or any other display items must not be distracting" (Intel ISEF, 2005, item 9). If you are unsure, consult your science teacher or other fair personnel ahead of time to learn more about how "distracting" might be interpreted in your particular situation. Be sure to have an alternative method of presentation prepared as a backup if there is even a small possibility that your child's display could be considered distracting.

Preparing for Judging

As the science fair approaches, take time to talk to your child about the judging process. Find out how he or she feels about it. Some students are quite self-possessed and enjoy talking about their work to anyone who will listen. Other students are quite nervous at the prospect of talking about their work with science fair judges, who they see as unknown adults and authority figures.

Usually, judges will have some time to examine the projects without the students present, and then will walk through and talk with students for 5 or 10 minutes each about their projects. Each student can expect to speak with two to four judges, who will come to the exhibit either individually or in small groups.

Science fair judges are volunteers who usually have a strong interest in the sciences themselves, and who want to encourage scientific interest among young students. The judges usually will try hard to put participants at ease, although they still will ask questions that can be difficult to answer. Stress to your child that it is all right to say that he is not sure about something and/or to ask the judges to clarify an unclear question. Your child will have some expertise in his or her project topic area by the time it is finished, but practice question and answer sessions are a good way for him or her to discover any knowledge gaps before the day of the fair. Some particularly alert teachers may schedule in-class interviews with peers for this purpose.

The judges have forms that they fill out to evaluate each project. Their evaluations are based on the project itself and on their talks with the student who conducted it. Judges do their best to provide constructive criticism and feedback to help students understand both the strengths and weaknesses of their work. The average scores obtained by each project determine which projects are awarded various prize ribbons. Some fairs, particularly

> Practicing interviews with teachers, neighbors, or other adults can help your student prepare for the judging process.

at the district, state, and national levels, also offer plaques, cash prizes, scholarships, and other incentives to the best work within particular project categories.

For students who intend to participate in the science fair over multiple years, observing projects done by others can be a great way to get new ideas for the following year. Encourage your child not only to examine others' efforts, but also to make notes in writing about what they like and what they might do differently if it were their project. Stress that the idea is not to borrow someone else's topic, but rather to share effective ideas. Notes can include anything from details of the exhibit board layout to how a particular question or topic was studied. Prize-winning projects, in particular, can be a good source of inspiration for future efforts.

Chapter 7

The Big Picture: Thinking About the Future

I t's a rare parent who hasn't wondered how his or her child's current interests will ever be converted into gainful employment. The compulsive and unusual interests of the scientifically motivated child sometimes call for more than the usual amount of faith that an appropriate niche is available.

Will your efforts be in vain if you child never becomes a scientist? Of course not. The skills and abilities you are encouraging in your son or daughter will always serve them well. Keep the faith! Things you can do right now will help. Here are some ideas to consider and potential pitfalls to avoid.

Connecting Science to Other Abilities

The good news is this—whether your child goes into science or some entirely different profession, being successful requires a diverse constellation of related abilities of the very sort that you have been cultivating with the help of the suggestions in this book.

Additionally, a host of careers require both scientific ability and other nonscientific skills. The scientific illustrator needs artistic ability, as well as a firm grounding in anatomy, botany, or other scientific fields to be able to understand and convey complex information using a visual format. The science writer or editor needs to understand a scientific field in depth to write about it effectively. The engineer making new medical devices must understand how people interact with machines in their environment, as well as how the machines themselves function. Developing a broad set of related interests can be useful in ways that are difficult to anticipate before they happen.

Specialized interests can also be relevant within scientific careers. This is particularly relevant to careers that are inherently interdisciplinary, such as archaeology, which may draw on everything from human physiology to botany, ancient languages, and analytical chemistry over the course of a single investigation. Because practicing scientists frequently need to draw on knowledge from other disciplines, children should always be encouraged to follow their interests toward whatever diverse skill combinations they may lead (Alexander, 2003).

Using Interest Inventories Wisely

Despite evidence that many or even most adults change jobs or careers during their working life, well-meaning adults tend to pressure children to make career choices early. For some children this may be no problem; a surprising number of students already have a clear career goal in mind from as early as age 13 (Achter, Lubinski, Benbow, & Eftekhari-Sanjani, 1999; Schmidt, Lubinski, & Benbow, 1998). Others may need a little more help. One tool that educators often use is an interest inventory. For links to a number of interest inventories, see http://www.paris95. k12.il.us/mayo/invent.html.

Interest inventories are designed to suggest vocational and career preferences. They generally are made up of long lists of traits that students rate as similar or dissimilar to their own interests, often in a comparative format that forces unnatural choices. Theoretically at least, by comparing students' interests to the interests expressed by successful individuals in a wide variety of careers, interest inventories can suggest appropriate fields of study that students otherwise might not have considered.

Interest inventories generally are considered appropriate for older students, usually at the high school and college level; however, some middle school students may also be interested to see what they can learn from such measures. School guidance counselors sometimes administer these inventories, and usually can also suggest other locations (such as employment offices or college career centers) where interested students can go to take them.

Interest inventories need to be taken with a proverbial grain of salt, however. They are not considered particularly accurate estimators of what students actually will end up doing, particularly for younger students whose awareness of career options may still be developing. Furthermore, interests and abilities are interrelated, and self-reported interests may be influenced by your child's current perceptions of his or her own abilities. Upon being asked to choose between two activities, as the inventories generally force the responder to do, most of us tend to choose not only the one that sounds more interesting but also the one we feel that we would do well on, based on how we view our current skills.

Interpreting inventory results to students also requires considerable awareness of potential personal and societal biases. For example, before the 1970s, many women (including my mother and aunt) whose test scores reported high interest in fields such as medicine and engineering were commonly told by counselors that these scores indicated flaws in the tests. One would like to believe that such biases no longer exist, but undoubtedly they do, although perhaps they are expressed in different ways today.

Interest inventories can limit your child's view of his or her future in another way, as well. Career paths suggested by such inventories also tend to be quite general, ignoring the great flexibility that exists in today's employment world. Within a broad category that can seem unsuitable or too challenging for a particular child's abilities there can be many niches that would suit just fine. For example, your highly verbal, socially precocious child might score as uninterested in becoming a veterinarian because her internal image is of an animal doctor with a private clinic. Yet, were she to know of veterinarians who work in the sales force of veterinary pharmaceutical companies, giving presentations on new products or developing scientifically accurate yet graphically interesting informative brochures, she might find the career to be a perfect match.

Talk to your child, both before and after he or she takes the inventory. Explain its usefulness and its limits. Most students, including your own child, have sufficient abilities and interests to succeed in a wide variety of career paths.

Putting it All Together

If you have read this book or even this chapter from start to finish, you may be feeling a bit overwhelmed by this point. Just by reading this book you've asked a great deal of yourself. With so much to sort out and make your own, it's sometimes hard to keep the larger picture in mind. Let's take a quick look at what this is all about.

There are really only a relatively few steps between potential scientific ability and demonstrated talent. Through your involvement, you hold the ability to make a profound difference in your child's life. Table 18 explores just a few of the ways you can make a difference.

Don't be afraid of your child's early achievement. No child is too young to do what he wants to do and can do safely. For instance, don't worry that your child might be ready for college at 16. (In actual studies on children of about equal brightness, some of whom started college earlier than 16 and some later, those who started college early were not only more likely to finish college but were also more likely to go on to highly successful careers in later life.) Take life as it comes.

Don't worry too much that you're not doing enough. Learning science is an ongoing process that will take the learner much of a lifetime to master. Keep in mind that research suggests that 10,000 hours of practice is a good (minimum) amount of practice necessary to reach high levels of performance in a field of study. The basics, as distilled in this book, offer a convenient port from which to begin helping your scientifically talented children embark on what will be a long and fascinating journey through a life in science. Soon enough, they will be sailing entirely on their own. Bon voyage!

**Table 18
Five Ways to Help Your Child Excel in Science**

1. Give your child lots of opportunities and encouragement within the family circle.
2. Give your child excellent individualized teaching, starting when he or she is very young.
3. Give your child opportunity for a great deal of practice, reward by advancement as quickly as achievement permits it.
4. Help your child be with others who share his or her interests and abilities.
5. Constantly give opportunities for real accomplishment at a young age.

Appendix: Additional Resources

lassroom experiences alone can't be expected to meet all the needs of your scientifically advanced son or daughter. You'll want and need to seek out additional enrichment opportunities beyond those mentioned so far. As an involved parent, you'll also want to further your own background knowledge because you know that will help you become even more effective with your child.

This appendix is offered as a bridge with which to enter a wide field of available opportunities. It identifies some well-respected traditional science- and technology-related competitions and programs, lists appropriate printed materials, as well as trustworthy Web-based resources, and gives a brief overview of each to help you decide whether it would be suitable for your particular child.

More Opportunities for Your Scientifically Advanced Child—and You!

Web Resources

One of the strongest ways to help a bright or talented child is simply to provide opportunities for a great deal of practice, rewarded by advancement as quickly as achievement permits. In addition to the many suggestions already offered in this book, consider encouraging your child to enter competitions such as those identified below.

Craftsman/NSTA Young Inventors Awards Program
http://www.nsta.org/programs/craftsman

The Young Inventors Awards Program competition is open to all students in grades 2–8. Students use their creative and mechanical abilities to invent or modify a tool to perform a useful function. Students must conceive and develop their ideas independently, but can have guidance from a parent or other adult to implement their invention. Prizes include savings bonds and merchandise from Sears retail stores.

Lucent Global Science Scholars Competition
http://www.iie.org/programs/lucent

The Lucent Global Science Scholars Program, in existence since 1999, is an annual academic competition sponsored by the Lucent Technologies Foundation for graduating seniors who demonstrate excellence in the sciences and plan to pursue a career in information and communications technologies. Recipients spend a week in Murray Hill, NJ, with researchers, scientists, and fellow Global Science Scholars at the headquarters of Lucent Technologies and Bell Labs, and receive a $5,000 award. Although this competition is for older students, it may provide a goal to strive toward for younger students.

Science Olympiad

http://www.soinc.org

The Science Olympiad is a nonprofit organization dedicated to improving science education in grades K–12 and student interest in science. The Science Olympiad conducts tournaments to encourage the attitude that science is exciting, and to promote teamwork, problem-solving skills, and a commitment to excellence in science achievement. More than 14,000 teams competed in Olympiad events in a recent year, from all 50 states and Canada. Competitions include divisions for students in elementary, middle, and high school grades as well as small schools and home school divisions.

Team America Rocketry Challenge

http://rocketcontest.org

The Aerospace Industries Association of America and the National Association of Rocketry sponsor an annual model rocketry competition for teams of students at the middle and high school level. For the 2005 competition, teams designed a rocket to safely launch an egg, returning it to Earth after a 60-second flight. Prizes include cash and savings bonds.

Toshiba NSTA ExploraVision Awards

http://www.exploravision.org

This competition for grades K–12 is conceptually driven. Students work in teams to investigate the history of a technology, envisage how the technology might change in the future, and suggest how society might be influenced by the projected changes. Regional winners design Web sites to promote their ideas. Top prizes are savings bonds.

Toy Challenge
http://www.toychallenge.com

This competition helps students learn about science, technology, and the design process by inventing and building a new toy. This is a team competition for groups of 3 to 8 students in grades 5–8, at least half of which must be girls. Teams work with an adult coach to develop their projects. Prizes include cash, travel, and science toys and games.

Web Sites

The Canadian Association for Girls in Science (CAGIS)
http://publish.uwo.ca/~cagis/testmap.htm

CAGIS' purpose is to support girls' interests in science, engineering, technology, and math. The organization, for girls ages 7–16, has clubs across Canada, a quarterly newsletter, and a password-protected "club house" where girls can discuss science-related interests with one another online. Some projects and other information are available without a password.

The Sally Ride Science Club™ (http://www.sallyrideclub.com) is a similar program operating in the United States.

The Chemical Heritage Foundation
http://www.chemheritage.org

The Chemical Heritage Foundation is an organization devoted to research, outreach, and interpretation related to the historical role of chemistry and chemical technology in society. The Foundation publishes *Chemical Heritage*, a newsmagazine of articles about historical developments in the chemical industries. Topics range from the development of Polaroid instant photography to the history of leaded gasoline. These articles offer an outstanding resource for older students who are learning about the history of technology or who are seeking inspiration for independent projects. The CHF Web site also includes links to classroom resources.

Girls Go Tech
http://www.girlsgotech.org

This initiative of the Girl Scouts of America is designed to increase girls' interest in learning about science, math, and technology. The Web site contains career information, some educational games, and links to a variety of Web sites and other resources for girls and their parents.

The Science House at North Carolina State University
http://www.science-house.org/info

This is a science learning resource site for parents, students, and teachers. It includes hands-on activities and curriculum materials, as well as links to summer programs for students and for science teachers. One link leads to the Middle School Physical Science Resource Center, which offers textbook reviews and other help specifically for teaching physical science to middle school students.

The Electronic Journal of Science Education
http://unr.edu/homepage/jcannon/ejse/ejse.html

This online journal publishes articles about science teaching and learning for teachers working with kindergarten through college-level students. This is a peer-reviewed and freely available source for locating research about specific topics in science education. (At the time of this writing, the journal's publishing schedule was backlogged to 2003.)

Printed Resources

Assouline, S., & Lupkowski-Shoplik, A. (2005). *Developing math talent: A guide for educating gifted and advanced learners in math.* Waco, TX: Prufrock Press.

Because scientific ability and mathematical ability are often closely related, you may find the recommendations in this book quite helpful when working with a child who is also mathematically talented. An entire chapter is devoted to advocacy and how parents can work with schools to meet their child's educational needs.

Barber, J., Buegler, M. E., Lowell, L., & Willard, C. (1988). *Discovering density.* Berkeley: Lawrence Hall of Science, University of California.

Barber, J., & Willard, C. (1994). *Bubble festival: Presenting bubble activities in a learning station format.* Berkeley: Lawrence Hall of Science, University of California.

These titles are only two samples of an extensive series of resources from the GEMS project at the Lawrence Hall of Science (for more, visit the Web site, http://www.lhsgems.org/gems.html).

Cothron, J. H., Giese, R. N., & Rezba, R. J. (2000). *Students and research: Practical strategies for science classrooms and competitions* (3rd ed.). Dubuque, IA: Kendall-Hunt Publishing Company.

This hefty paperback volume offers a comprehensive overview of experimental design, data analysis, project management, and competition preparedness for anyone involved with student research projects. There are also a number of experimental activities that may be used to familiarize students with the research process before they undertake more independent work. The material covering introductory statistics is not readily available elsewhere. The book is aimed primarily at secondary students, although parts may be applicable to middle school, as well as college-level learners.

Csikszentmihalyi, M., Rathunde, K., and Whalen, S. (with Wong, M.). (1997). *Talented teenagers: The roots of success and failure*. Cambridge: Cambridge University Press.

This study followed more than 200 talented adolescents throughout several years to learn why some became successful while others retreated into mediocrity and underachievement. While not specific to science talent alone, the chapter discussing how families influence the development of talent is particularly worth examining for parents who want to increase their children's odds of becoming successful adults.

Elson, L. M. (1982). *The zoology coloring book*. New York: Barnes & Noble Books.

This book is just one in a series, mostly in the biological disciplines, that teach science through the coloring of detailed and well-labeled anatomical drawings. Because older students often find mastering new vocabulary to be the most difficult obstacle to scientific learning, these books fill an important need. The labels can help satisfy the scientifically inclined child's need to name things, and the drawings provide a useful introductory activity before dissections or other studies of anatomical specimens. I have used selected pages from these books successfully with students as young as the third grade.

Epp, D. N. (1995). *The chemistry of natural dyes.* Middletown, OH: Terrific Science Press.

This short book presents laboratory activities and explanations that can be used by a teacher or parent to introduce students to the chemistry of natural dyes. The introduction also offers an annotated list of publications and other resources available through The Center for Chemistry Education at Miami University. Links connecting book activities to the National Science Education Standards are available on the center's Web site, http://www.terrificscience.org.

Feldman, R. D. (2000). *Whatever happened to the Quiz Kids? The perils and profits of growing up gifted.* Lincoln, NE: iUniverse.

The Quiz Kids, stars of the popular show of the same name in the 1940s and 50s, were tracked down decades later to see what had become of them as adults. The author, herself a former Quiz Kid and today a grandmother, tells what became of her companions from the show. Although there is little that concerns science learning directly, the text is captivating and it has implications for how—as well as how not—to raise talented children today.

Kellett, M. (2005). *How to develop children as researchers: A step-by-step guide to teaching the research process.* London: Paul Chapman Publishing.

This book offers a practice-based approach to teaching research skills to children. The author suggests that research is appropriate for all students ages 12–14, and for scientifically precocious children as young as ages 9–10. Although a handful of examples are from the UK context and may be less familiar to readers in the United States, as a whole this book will be quite valuable to parents, teachers, and even students themselves who are working on an independent research project.

Kipnis, N. (1993). *Rediscovering optics.* Minneapolis, MN: BENA Press.

Kipnis approaches scientific learning by having students conduct optical experiments through which they can repeat historical discoveries. He recommends that these activities be done at home, as well as in school, because experimentation at home allows students more time and creative latitude than is possible in school. The book is most suitable for older (high school) students, but with careful adult guidance some of the activities could be appropriate for younger ages.

Lowery, L. F. (1985). *The everyday science sourcebook.* Palo Alto, CA: Dale Seymour Publications.

Hundreds of teaching and learning activities are outlined and presented by topic area, within a framework designed to emphasize the interrelationships among ideas. This book should prove particularly useful as a learning guide for the parent or student who already has some background knowledge in science.

McCormack, A. J. (1990). *Magic and showmanship for teachers.* Riverview, FL: Idea Factory.

This fascinating book presents magic tricks that teachers can use to enhance their classroom instruction. Tricks are grouped into chapters by classes, such as science, math, and art, and each chapter contains from 3–14 relevant tricks. Magic tricks can help develop students' observational skills, which are quite important in scientific learning, and many also are simple enough that children can learn to perform the tricks themselves.

Ostlund, K. L. (1992). *Science process skills: Assessing hands-on student performance.* Menlo Park, CA: Addison-Wesley.

Process skills are abilities such as observing, measuring, or predicting that are used for creating and making sense of information about the world. This book provides a list of science process skills and gives hands-on activities for developing and assessing these skills. Activities are arranged by difficulty into six levels, corresponding roughly to grades K–5

Rimm, S. (2003). *See Jane win for girls: A smart girl's guide to success.* Minneapolis, MN: Free Spirit Publishing.

Rimm and her daughters surveyed more than a thousand successful women to find out how they got that way. This book distills the findings in the form of recommendations written for girls at the upper elementary and middle school level. Science-oriented recommendations are limited, but all girls may find Rimm's other advice helpful.

Smutny, J. F., Walker, S. Y., & Meckstroth, E. A. (1997). *Teaching young gifted children in the regular classroom: Identifying, nurturing, and challenging ages 4–9.* Minneapolis, MN: Free Spirit Publishing.

Although written for teachers, this book is full of suggestions that parents will find useful. Helpful topics addressed include identifying giftedness, documenting students' development, and building parent-school partnerships. Chapter 6 gives strategies for promoting discovery and higher-level thinking in math and science, and an annotated bibliography includes 32 books and resource materials in science for students with interests in this area.

Sternberg, R. J., & Grigorenko, E. L. (2000). *Teaching for successful intelligence: To increase student learning and achievement.* Arlington Heights, IL: SkyLight Professional Development.

The authors describe Sternberg's well-known three-part theory of successful intelligence, and present examples and lessons that illustrate teaching strategies designed to develop each aspect. The section on analytical intelligence may be the most directly relevant to science learning, although the authors believe that all three aspects are important for achieving success in life.

Thier, M., & Daviss, B. (2002). *The new science literacy: Using language skills to help students learn science.* Portsmouth, NH: Heinemann.

The authors describe how to teach science through guided inquiry, using language and literacy skills to help students develop their scientific abilities. Elementary, middle, and secondary levels are considered. Because many scientifically inclined students possess strong language skills, these techniques are quite relevant to science learning, as well.

Trombley, L. (1985). *Mastering the Periodic Table: Exercises on the elements.* Portland, ME: J. Weston Walch.

The Periodic Table of the Elements forms the backbone of the discipline of chemistry and is an integral part of many other branches of science and technology. This brief book consists of crossword puzzles, word finds, and other activities for students who are learning the elements. The pages are designed as masters to be photocopied.

References

Achter, J. A., Lubinski, D., Benbow, C. P., & Eftekhari-Sanjani, H. (1999). Assessing vocational preference among gifted adolescents adds incremental validity to abilities: A discriminant analysis of educational outcomes over a 10-year interval. *Journal of Educational Psychology, 91,* 777–786.

Alexander, P. A. (2003). The development of expertise: The journey from acclimation to proficiency. *Educational Researcher, 32*(8), 10–14.

Allchin, D. (2001). Error types. *Perspectives on Science, 9,* 38–59.

American Association for the Advancement of Science. (1993). *Benchmarks for science literacy: Project 2061.* New York: Oxford University Press.

American Association for the Advancement of Science. (1999). *Dialogue on early childhood science, mathematics, and technology education.* New York: Oxford University Press.

American Association for the Advancement of Science. (2001). *Designs for science literacy.* New York: Oxford University Press.

American Association of University Women. (1991). *Shortchanging girls, shortchanging America*. Retrieved October 27, 2005, from http://www.aauw.org/research/SGSA.pdf

American Association of University Women. (1998). *Gender gaps: Where schools still fail our children*. Washington, DC: Author.

American Psychological Association. (2001). *Publication manual of the American Psychological Association* (5th ed.). Washington, DC: Author.

Assouline, S. G., Colangelo, N., Lupkowski-Shoplik, A. E., Lipscomb, J., & Forstadt, L. (2003). *Iowa acceleration scale 2nd edition: A guide to whole-grade acceleration K–8*. Scottsdale, AZ: Great Potential Press.

Bloom, B. (1985). *Developing talent in young people*. New York: Ballantine.

Bybee, R. W., & Sund, R. B. (1990). *Piaget for educators* (2nd ed.). Prospect Heights, NJ: Waveland Press.

Campbell, P. B., & Clewell, B. C. (1999). Science, math, and girls. Still a long way to go. *Education Week, 19*(2), 50–51.

Carroll, R. T. (2005). *Clever Hans phenomenon*. Retrieved October 27, 2005, from http://www.skepdic.com/cleverhans.html

Colangelo, N., Assouline, S. G., & Gross, M. U. M. (2004). *A nation deceived: How schools hold back America's brightest students* (Vols. 1 & 2). Iowa City: The Connie Belin & Jacqueline N. Blank International Center for Gifted Education and Talent Development.

Cothron, J. H., Giese, R. N., & Rezba, R. J. (2000). *Students and research: Practical strategies for science classrooms and competitions* (3rd ed.). Dubuque, IA: Kendall-Hunt Publishing Company.

Cramond, B. (2005). *Fostering creativity in gifted students*. Waco, TX: Prufrock Press.

Davalos, R. A., & Haensly, P. A. (1997). After the dust has settled: Youth reflect on their high school mentored research experience. *Roeper Review, 19*, 204–207.

Davidson Institute for Talent Development. (2005). *How parent advocacy groups can make a difference: An interview with Christine Smith, Southlake Parents for Academic Excellence (SPACE).* Retrieved March 24, 2005, from http://www.geniusdenied.com/articles/record. aspx?NavID=13_0&rid=13877

Deal, L. (2003). *The boredom solution: Understanding and dealing with boredom.* San Luis Obispo, CA: Dandy Lion Publications.

Delisle, J. R. (2003, November). *Highly gifted, barely served: The legacy of inclusion.* Paper presented at the 50th annual convention of the National Association for Gifted Children, Indianapolis, IN.

Ensign, J. (1997). *Homeschooling gifted students: An introductory guide for parents.* Reston, VA: ERIC Clearinghouse on Disabilities and Gifted Education. (ERIC Document Reproduction Service No. ED414683)

Feynman, R. P. (1974). *Cargo cult science: From a Caltech commencement address.* Retrieved October 27, 2005, from http://www.physics.brocku.ca/etc/cargo_cult_science.html

Feynman, R. P. (as told to R. Leighton). (1985). *Surely you're joking, Mr. Feynman: Adventures of a curious character.* New York: W. W. Norton & Co.

Gagné, F. (2004). An imperative, but, alas, improbable consensus. *Roeper Review, 27*, 12–14.

Great Explorations in Math and Science (GEMS). (1993). *Connecting young people's literature to great explorations in math and science.* Berkeley, CA: Lawrence Hall of Science.

Hargittai, I. (2003, Spring). Alan MacDiarmid. *Chemical Heritage, 21*, 8–11.

Hébert, T. P. (2005). *Inventions and inventing for gifted students.* Waco, TX: Prufrock Press.

Hershberger, R. (2000). *Science process skills lecture hall.* Retrieved October 27, 2005, from http://www.rickhershberger.com/bio-activesite/elemsci/lecturehall/process_skills.pdf

Hertzog, N. (2003). Advocacy: On the cutting edge. *Gifted Child Quarterly, 47*, 66–81.

Hubisz, J. L. (2003, May). Middle-school texts don't make the grade. *Physics Today,* 50–54.

Inhelder, B., & Piaget, J. (1958). *The growth of logical thinking from childhood to adolescence.* New York: Basic Books.

Intel ISEF. (2005). *General Intel ISEF information and requirements.* Retrieved October 27, 2005, from http://www.sciserv.org/isef/students/rules/safdisp.asp

Johnsen, S. K., Haensly, P. A., Ryser, G. R., & Ford, R. F. (2002). Changing general education classroom practices to adapt for gifted students. *Gifted Child Quarterly, 46*, 45–63.

Joyce, B. A., & Farenga, S. (2000). Young girls in science: Academic ability, perceptions, and future participation in science. *Roeper Review, 22*, 261–262.

Kearney, K. (2004). *Gifted children and homeschooling: An annotated bibliography.* Retrieved November 7, 2005, from www.dirhody.com/discanner/gifthome.html

Kellett, M. (2005). *How to develop children as researchers: A step-by-step guide to teaching the research process.* Thousand Oaks, CA: Sage Publications.

Kipnis, N. (1993). *Rediscovering optics.* Minneapolis, MN: BENA Press.

Matthews, M. S. (2004). Understanding achievement tests. *Duke Gifted Letter, 5*(1), 6.

Matthews, R. W., Koballa, T. R., Flage, L. R., & Pyle, E. J. (1996). *WOWBugs: New life for life science.* Athens, GA: Riverview Press.

Mullis, I. V. S., & Jenkins, L. B. (1988). *The science report card.* Princeton, NJ: Educational Testing Service.

National Academy of Sciences. (1996). *National science education standards.* Retrieved December, 13, 2005, from http://books.nap.edu/html/nses/html/overview.html#content

No Child Left Behind Act, 20 U.S.C. §6301 (2001).

Olszewski-Kubilius, P. (1998). Research evidence regarding the validity and effects of talent search educational programs. *Journal of Secondary Gifted Education, 9,* 134–142.

Ostlund, K. L. (1992). *Science process skills: Assessing hands-on student performance.* Menlo Park, CA: Addison-Wesley Publishing.

Padilla, M. J. (1990). *The science process skills* (Research Monograph No. 9004). Burnaby, BC, Canada: National Association for Research in Science Teaching.

Passow, A. H. (1988). School, university, laboratory, and museum cooperation in identifying and nurturing potential scientists. In P. F. Brandwein, A. H. Passow, D. C. Fort, & G. Skoog (Eds.), *Gifted young in science: Potential through performance* (pp. 245–254). Washington, DC: National Science Teachers Association.

Princiotta, D., Bielick, S., & Chapman, C. (2004). 1.1 million home-schooled students in the United States in 2003. *Educational Statistics Quarterly, 6*(3). Retrieved November 7, 2005, from http://nces.ed.gov/programs/quarterly/vol_6/6_3/index.asp

Rakow, S. J. (1988). The gifted in middle school science. In P. F. Brandwein, A. H. Passow, D. C. Fort, & G. Skoog (Eds.), *Gifted young in science: Potential through performance* (pp. 141–154). Washington, DC: National Science Teachers Association.

Reis, S. M., & Renzulli, J. S. (2005). *Curriculum compacting: An easy start to differentiating for high-potential students.* Waco, TX: Prufrock Press.

Reis, S. M., Westburg, K. L., Kulikowich, J., Caillard, F., Hébert, T., Plucker, J., et al. (1993). *Why not let high ability students start school in January? The curriculum compacting study* (Research Monograph No. RM93106). Storrs, CT: National Research Center on the Gifted and Talented. (ERIC Document Reproduction Service No. ED379847)

Rogers, K. B. (2005, April). *The accountability of education plans for gifted learners.* Paper presented at the annual meeting of the American Educational Research Association, Montreal, QC, Canada.

Roseman, J. E., Kesidou, S., Stern, L., & Caldwell, A. (1999). Heavy books light on learning: AAAS Project 2061 evaluates middle grades science textbooks. *Science Books and Films, 35,* 243–247.

Rudner, L. M. (1999). *Scholastic achievement and demographic characteristics of home school students in 1998.* Retrieved November 7, 2005, from http://epaa.asu.edu/epaa/v7n8

Rutherford, F. J., & Ahlgren, A. (1990). Science for all Americans. New York: Oxford University Press.

Runco, M. A. (2004). Creativity. *Annual Review of Psychology, 55,* 657–687.

Schmidt, D. B., Lubinski, D., & Benbow, C. P. (1998). Validity of assessing educational-vocational preference dimensions among intellectually talented 13-year-olds. *Journal of Counseling Psychology, 45,* 436–453.

Siegel, J., & Shaughnessy, M. F. (1991). *Gifted females can be supported in math and science: A proposal for mentoring in secondary schools.* Reston, VA: ERIC Clearinghouse on Disabilities and Gifted Education. (ERIC Document Reproduction Service No. ED344381)

Simpson, R. D., & Oliver, J. S. (1985). Attitudes toward science and achievement motivation profiles of male and female science students in grades six through ten. *Science Education, 69*, 511–526.

Sloane, K. D. (1985). Home influences on talent development. In B. S. Bloom (Ed.), *Developing talent in young people* (pp. 439–476). New York: Ballantine.

Smutny, J. F., Walker, S. Y., & Meckstroth, E. A. (1997). *Teaching young gifted children in the regular classroom: Identifying, nurturing, and challenging ages 4–9*. Minneapolis, MN: Free Spirit Publishing.

Solochek, J. S. (2005, March 1). Poor schools face more cuts: No Child Left Behind forces schools to redirect their spending, dropping programs. *St. Petersburg Times*. Retrieved November 7, 2005, from http://www.sptimes.com/2005/03/01/Hillsborough/Poor_schools_face_mor.shtml

Stanley, J. (1978). SMPY's DT-PI model: Diagnostic testing followed by prescriptive instruction. *Intellectually Talented Youth Bulletin, 4*(10), 7–8.

Stanley, J. (1998, May). *Helping students learn only what they don't already know*. Paper presented at the Fourth Biennial Henry B. & Jocelyn Wallace National Research Symposium on Talent Development, The University of Iowa, Iowa City.

Starko, A. J. (2005). *Creativity in the classroom: Schools of curious delight* (3rd ed.). Mahwah, NJ: Lawrence Erlbaum Associates.

Sternberg, R. J. (2004). Good intentions, bad results: A dozen reasons why the No Child Left Behind Act is failing our schools. *Education Week, 24*(9), 42, 56.

Subotnik, R. F., & Arnold, K. D. (1995). Passing through the gates: Career establishment of talented women scientists. *Roeper Review, 18*, 55–61.

Subotnik, R. F., Stone, K. M., & Steiner, C. (2001). Lost generation of elite talent in science. *Journal of Secondary Gifted Education, 13*, 33–43.

Talton, E. L., & Simpson, R. D. (1985). Relationships between peer and individual attitudes toward science among adolescent students. *Science Education, 69*(1), 19–24.

Taylor, B. A. P., Poth, J., & Portman, D. J. (1995). *Teaching physics with toys: Activities for grades K–9.* Desoto, TX: McGraw-Hill.

Thier, M., & Daviss, B. (2002). *The new science literacy: Using language skills to help students learn science.* Portsmouth, NH: Heinemann.

Torrance, E. P. (1968). A longitudinal examination of the fourth-grade slump in creativity. *Gifted Child Quarterly, 12*, 195–199.

Torrance, E. P. (1983). *The manifesto for children.* Athens, GA: Georgia Studies of Creative Behavior and Full Circle Counseling.

U.S. Department of Education, Office of Educational Research and Improvement. (1993). *National excellence: A case for developing America's talent.* Washington, DC: U.S. Government Printing Office.

Winner, E. (1997). Exceptionally high intelligence and schooling. *American Psychologist, 52*, 1070–1081.

About the Author

Michael S. Matthews, Ph.D., is an assistant professor in the Gifted Education Program of the Department of Special Education at the University of South Florida in Tampa. He holds a Ph.D. in educational psychology, with a concentration in gifted and creative education, from the University of Georgia. Prior to coming to USF, he was a postdoctoral research fellow at the Duke University Talent Identification Program. Before his doctoral studies at the University of Georgia, Dr. Matthews had been in turn a high school science teacher, a laboratory chemist, and an archaeologist.

Dr. Matthews is a regular presenter at state, national, and international meetings on gifted education. He is also the 2006 program chair for the special interest group, Research on Giftedness and Talent, of the American Educational Research Association. He serves as a reviewer for journals that include the *Gifted Child Quarterly*, the *Journal of Secondary Gifted Education*, the *Journal for the Education of the Gifted*, and the *Journal of Chemical Education*. At the University of South Florida, Dr.

Matthews teaches graduate classes on giftedness and creativity. His research interests include underachievement, science education, and varied issues related to cultural and linguistic diversity in gifted education.